IRON WILL

IRON WILL

AN AMPUTEE'S JOURNEY TO ATHLETIC EXCELLENCE

RODERICK SEWELL
with KAREN HUNTER

LEGACY
LIT

New York

Legacy Lit, an imprint of Hachette Books
Hachette Book Group
1290 Avenue of the Americas
New York, NY 10104
HachetteBookGroup.com
X.com/LegacyLitBooks
Instagram.com/LegacyLitBooks

First Edition: August 2025

Grand Central Publishing is a division of Hachette Book Group, Inc. The Legacy Lit and Grand Central Publishing names and logos are trademarks of Hachette Book Group, Inc.

The Hachette Speakers Bureau provides a wide range of authors for speaking events.

To find out more, go to www.hachettespeakersbureau.com or call (866) 376-6591.

The publisher is not responsible for websites (or their content) that are not owned by the publisher.

Print book interior design by Taylor Navis.

Library of Congress Cataloging-in-Publication Data has been applied for.

ISBNs: 978-1-5387-4156-6 (hardcover); 978-1-5387-4209-9 (ebook)

Printed in the United States of America

LSC-C

10 9 8 7 6 5 4 3 2 1

To Mom.

And to the Jackson, the Sewells, my family and friends who contributed to making me the man I am today.

Epigraph TK

Contents

CONTENTS

Introduction

FIRE

Smoke filled the air. Chaos and fear. Bottles thrown. Things set on fire. Stores looted and destroyed. People were screaming and crying. Hurt and rage mingled with the smoke and fire.

This was the day I came into the world. April 29, 1992: the day the Los Angeles Riots broke out.

It was the day that four white police officers were found not guilty of beating Rodney King, a Black man, half to death. It was yet another day that Black people across the country felt the sting of the injustice of that "not guilty" verdict, brought forth by an all-white jury. Civilians and news outlets alike replayed the beating of King—one of the first such incidents caught on film. And while protestors took to the streets and Los Angeles went up in flames, little fires burned throughout the nation in the hearts and minds of people who saw that verdict as yet another punch in the face.

While most of the nation watched the unrest of the Los Angeles Riots unfold, a little more than a hundred and twenty miles away in San Diego, California, my mother was in labor.

I arrived at the peak of the riots, into a world that was on fire on two fronts.

"You *would* decide to come on that day of all days," my mother laughed with me years later as she shared how everyone was glued to the television watching the riots. But for her, all she could focus on was me...and the pain she was in.

My mother had six miscarriages before getting pregnant with me. She had all but given up on having a child when she found out she was pregnant again. She saw me, barely formed, as her miracle. That was until the pain started in the first couple of months.

"Here we go again," she thought as she held her breath with each passing trimester, wondering if this would be the one that took me away. The pain and fear made it impossible to relax and enjoy her pregnancy. There was also my dad. He was physically around for most of the pregnancy but wasn't there much financially. A former military officer, he struggled to keep a paycheck, which compounded his need to be in the streets hanging out, often with other women.

My mom *had* to work, so she did. Right up until the final weeks.

Mama worked for the Department of Defense for the US

government doing what would be considered "man's work." She cut asbestos and lifted the heavy boxes of material onto naval ships and into containers headed for naval shipyards for vessels like the USS *Abraham* or the USS *Kitty Hawk*.

Back then, asbestos was used in planes, radar stations, and on bases where servicemembers were stationed. It was used as insulation in aircrafts, heat shields, and durable valves, gaskets, electrical wiring, and brakes—you name it. My mother's job was to stack the reams of asbestos, which weighed anywhere from fifty to seventy pounds, by hand, onto the palate. After the palate was full, she would then have to move them onto the shipping containers with a forklift. Yes, my mother operated a forklift! She was one of three women doing this job.

"You should have seen me, Roderick. I was better at it than most of the men!" she would brag.

She didn't tell her bosses she was pregnant because they were reluctant to hire women for that exact reason. Management, of course, eventually found out. But she never took a single day off or called in sick, and she never complained. She showed up and worked. Hard.

There was no paid maternity leave in 1992. We were still in the Reagan era, and the resources that were promised to trickle down from the top weren't getting to us. When Bill Clinton was elected president of the United States later that year, one of his first domestic priorities was signing into law the Family and Medical Leave Act, but that wasn't until 1993.

So, my mom worked and concealed her pregnancy until she couldn't hide it. The higher ups were not happy when they found out, but she assured them she would work until she couldn't any-more. And that's what she did. She worked that forklift until her seventh month, when they finally moved her to a paper-pushing role behind a desk. She worked diligently through the morning sickness, which carried over into afternoon sickness. She worked through the pain, which seemed to get more severe in the later months.

"I didn't have a choice," she told me. If she didn't work, she didn't get paid. "Them diapers weren't going to pay for themselves."

The pain in her belly was so constant, Mama told me, that she became numb to it. But when the sharp pain in her stomach moved down to her pelvis, she knew she had to go get it checked out.

"You were an active baby…a very active baby," my mother would later tell me, the way she tells me everything—in passing and matter of fact. She shared things, it seemed, as if she was telling me so that *she* wouldn't forget. I didn't ask her questions, probably because I knew she was sure to volunteer information whenever it struck her.

Her doctor was an older white man at the local teaching hospital in a poorer area of San Diego where most of the patients were Black and Hispanic. Before the vast studies on how the medical field ignores pregnant Black women's pain, my mother lived through it. After briefly examining her, the doctor told my mother he could find no issue. He told her that her pain was normal, and he even accused her of overreacting and being a bit of a hypochondriac.

"He told me I was exaggerating," Mama told me.

She went back to work and pushed through the pain, which had gotten so bad at times that she could hardly walk. Some of the pain, I'm sure, was caused by my activity in the womb.

"The whole pregnancy you were kicking—actually punching—me. I had bruises all over my tummy."

But she also sensed, though, that something else was wrong.

"Doc, I *really* think something is off," she pleaded with him on her next visit.

"Let's do a sonogram. You'll see that you have nothing to be concerned with," he said.

She had had a sonogram earlier in the pregnancy, and everything looked fine. But when the doctor printed out this one and handed it to her, she could see something was different. There was a cloudy spot in the area where my legs should be.

"See right here," my mom pointed to the cloudy area. "This looks okay to you?"

"Those are just normal shadows," the doctor said bushing her off. "Your baby is fine."

He's the doctor, my mother thought. *He has to know more than I do...right?*

So, she went back to work...in pain!

Two weeks before I was born, Mom's pain was so bad that my dad, who'd decided to stick around for the final weeks of the pregnancy, rushed her to the hospital. My mother thought that she was having contractions and that it was time. But the doctor sent her back home telling her they were Braxton Hicks—false contractions.

It was around one in the afternoon on April 29, when her water officially broke.

Hours later, America broke too.

———

At 3:15 in the afternoon—after seven days of deliberation—an all-white jury acquitted Sgt. Stacey Koon, and Officers Theodore Briseno, Laurence Powell, and Timothy Wind in the brutal beating of Rodney King. For a little more than a year, Black America had been holding its collective breath waiting for justice. In March 1991, an eighty-nine-second VHS video was released to the public of King, a Black man who had been involved in a traffic stop that escalated. He is seen in the video lying face down on the ground surrounded by about ten police officers. One of the officers stomps on his head, and as King moves to shield himself from further blows you can see other officers start to tee off on him with billy clubs. It looks as if they are in batting practice for the Los Angeles Dodgers. The kicks, the blows, the electrical volt from the tasers—so much violence in such a short period of time. The image of King's face in the aftermath, bloated and bloody, immediately incited a rallying cry for justice across the country.

But following the not guilty verdict, Black America reached a critical point that was bigger than Rodney King. Such public brutality against one Black person is rarely an isolated incident in our community. Just as the protests for George Floyd during the summer of 2020 were also about Ahmaud Arbery and Breonna Taylor, Trayvon Martin and Eric Garner, Sandra Bland and Tamir Rice, the reaction to Rodney King was also about Latasha Harlins.

Weeks after the Rodney King beating, fifteen-year-old Latasha Harlins was shot in the back of the head by a convenience store owner in Los Angeles. The shop owner had accused Harlins of stealing. Was it because Latasha Harlins was Black? Harlins believed so, and a verbal altercation became physical when the shop owner grabbed Harlins' by the sweater and snatched her backpack. Harlins hit the shop owner, who then threw a stool at her. As Harlins attempted to flee the store, she was shot in the back of the head.

That video from the security footage of the shooting came out just days following the King video.

The shop owner, Soon Ja Du, was found guilty of voluntary manslaughter by a jury, but the judge, Joyce Ann Karlin, gave her a suspended sentence. Du got off with community service and a $500 fine. (According to published reports, Judge Karlin had previously given a man who kicked a dog a stiffer sentence).

No justice, no peace! became the rallying cry. The outrage was building in a city already in the throes of a crack cocaine epidemic, which gave birth to a rise in gang violence. Hip-hop and rap chronicled the rage—from Ice T's "Cop Killer" to NWA's "F tha Police."

I may not have grown up loving these songs, but I surely knew about them.

By April, Los Angeles was a powder keg, and the verdict in favor of the police, coupled with the slap on the wrist for the killer of Latasha Harlins, lit the fuse.

As my dad pulled up to the hospital with my mom, another man, Reginald Dennis, was being pulled from his truck in the middle of the riots and beaten. Helicopters and news cameras captured everything. The fire was raging.

My mother was wheeled into the hospital hollering. My father was a nervous wreck and didn't know how to help. The doctors were suddenly urgent and attentive after seeing the latest scans.

The umbilical cord was wrapped around my neck, and I was dying. My heartbeat was faint. They had to rush my mother into surgery for an emergency Cesarean.

It was a teaching hospital in a low-income neighborhood in San Diego, and it may not have been totally prepared for this moment. They allowed my father in the room in scrubs. But he didn't last past the first incision into my mother's stomach. The cut was rough, and lower than it should have been (making my mom's recovery all the more difficult). And there was a *lot* of blood. My dad was excited to have his firstborn son (he already had a daughter, we later discovered, from a previous relationship). But he never got to see me born. He hit the floor at the first sight of all that blood. Passed out cold. They carried him out of the operating room.

I arrived around nine that evening. By this time, just about everything in South Central was ablaze.

My mother was unconscious for my arrival. She didn't get to see me until hours later, in recovery. By then, they knew that the cloud on the ultrasound wasn't just shadows. My mother's intuition was right.

By the time she first held me, she knew she would have to prepare me for more than being a Black boy in a world that may see me as a Rodney King.

Chapter One

THE FIRST LEG: THE SWIM

THE WATER WAS FREEZING. IT TOOK MY BREATH AS I DOVE IN. And then a calm washed over me.

As the sun was cresting over the horizon in Kona, Hawaii, I started the first leg of my long journey—the Ironman World Championships. If I crossed the finish line, I would become the first above-the-knee double amputee to do so. But I first had to finish this 2.4-mile swim.

This was the first year the organizers of the Ironman decided to send the swimmers out in waves. There were more than two thousand competitors, and having us swim all together at once would have been difficult to manage. So, the abled men started their swim at 6:25 a.m., followed by the abled women at 6:30 a.m., then the swimmers with disabilities at 6:35. For months I had trained for the initial rush into the water, the failing arms and legs, dodging the kicks and strokes of other swimmers. I was actually looking forward to it.

Most of the physically challenged racers were either strong cyclists or strong runners, skills we all needed to make it through the second and third legs of the triathlon. Me though? I was a Paralympic swimmer. *This* was my race. I was one of the best, if not the best, swimmers with disabilities in this race, and I knew it.

By the time of the Ironman race, I had already swum for Team USA on three national teams, swimming 5,000 to 10,000 meters regularly. I won gold in the 100-meter breaststroke in my first national team event, in 2014. In 2015, I won bronze in the 100-meter breaststroke. My last competition was in 2017, when we won bronze in the medley relay, I swam the freestyle leg. Even when I wasn't preparing to compete, I stayed in the water as much as I could since I was a kid. Short of being born a fish, no other physically challenged swimmer in the water that day had more experience in the swim than me. The water was my happy place, and I especially enjoyed being in open water with a crowd. I had conquered my fear of it, and now it was the place that would allow me to conquer my life. A place where I found courage and achievement. And freedom. I trained for that.

I had not trained for the solitude.

I took off so quickly in the swim that within the first ten minutes, I was swimming alone. I was so far ahead of the other physically disabled swimmers that I couldn't hear them splashing behind me. And the women, who started five minutes before me were also out of sight up ahead.

In the silence of the open water, I cleared my mind. I appreciated the stillness as I settled into a routine, *pull, pull, pull,* moving on auto-pilot. There was a time when being in the ocean would have sent me into sheer panic. There was a time when I would not even be able to go near the water without breaking down.

But the fear, along with my competitors, was far behind me. I had trained to be in a pack for this first leg of Ironman. Now I had to come up with a new game plan. I had to find the turnaround buoys and map out my course without the benefit of following others.

I had spent months training in the Endless Pool at my work-out facility, Tailwind Endurance, in New York City on West Seventy-Second. All summer 2019, I got to use the Endless Pool whenever I wanted and after my coaching sessions. I coached endurance athletes, and I was tough. They listened to me because I was faster than they were, and I didn't have legs. I also trained at the Jewish Community Center (JCC) on West Seventy-Sixth Street and Amsterdam. They had a beautiful pool on the fifth floor with amazing views of the city. I taught a swim class for adults, mostly triathletes, at the JCC every Tuesday night, and I trained there three times a week.

In the Endless Pool, I got the exact push I needed from the jets, which mirrored the currents of open water. I learned how to fight against the pressurized water and find calm and rhythm in chaos. At the JCC, I trained in the crowded pool navigating the kicks and strokes of other swimmers. I preferred training at the JCC because they also had a steam room and accessible showers right outside the pool. It was like a country club.

I didn't, however, train for the solitude—for being in the open sea alone. I couldn't prepare for this version of the ocean. No matter how big the pool, you were never too far from another person. In the ocean, there was unlimited room. And I didn't anticipate the strength of the currents. The constant push and pull came with more force than I was used to. As high tech as it was, the Endless Pool could not simulate this.

Rule number 1 in ocean swimming—don't fight the current. It's like life—you need to go with the flow.

In the ocean, getting farther faster is all about technique and strength. Thanks to my first swim instructor, Alan Voisard, I had both. The power in swimming comes from your legs, the kick. That wasn't an option for me. So I had to use my hips and core to stay above the water so that I could transfer the power using my arm strength. While the breaststroke was my best, for the Ironman race, the freestyle would be most effective. I had to strike, stretch and extend, and pull while I rotated my hips to catch a breath.

Strike, extend, pull, rotate, breathe.

Strike, extend, pull, rotate, breathe.

Strike, extend, pull, rotate, breathe.

The rhythm and consistency were like following a drumbeat in the water. When the water got choppy, which it did, I had to widen my arms. I used my arms as rotors, with the tips of my fingers as my navigators. I had been training for months, but really, I had been training for most of my life. This was an endurance race. You finished by not stopping.

I had to navigate not only the pull of the currents but also the complete loneliness.

I was a little nervous being alone. Anything could happen in the open ocean. The competition reps used only overhead drones to keep track of competitors. When I was young, the thought of being alone in the open water was terrifying, even with my growing confidence in swimming. Once I got strong enough to swim in the open water, I always swam in a pack of people or with a guide. But never alone. In my mind, I just knew dark meat was a delicacy to these sea creatures. In a pack, if there were sharks or other predators, I wouldn't be the biggest, most tasty option. I knew to stay in the middle of the pack like a baby elephant.

But here I was exposed. Alone. Afraid.

I thought about slowing down so that I could swim just ahead of the crowd. But I had to remind myself why I was there: to win! That meant finishing in the seventeen-hour cutoff time. Swimming, my best event, was my best chance to do that. If I didn't finish first here, I may not finish the entire race in time.

My game plan was to catch up to at least one abled woman who had started ten minutes before I did. Just one woman. Instead of slowing down, I sped up.

I discovered on this day that my drive and will to finish this race was greater than my fear.

———

The first time I swam in the ocean, I was eleven years old. Alan Voisard, one of the most incredible swim coaches alive, was the one who taught me to swim. But he told me if I wanted to swim competitively, I needed to tackle the ocean. That was a whole new level of fear. But I trusted him.

After just a few months of swimming lessons at the pool, he asked me, "Are you ready to go to the next level?" *No!* I wasn't ready. He wasn't really asking the question, though. Alan's style was no non-sense, encouraging, and tough. He didn't baby me. He never let me off the hook. So, when he said, *Are you ready to go to the next level?*, he didn't wait for a response. He knew I was ready. As encouraging as Alan was with his words, he was the kind of instructor who believed in a healthy challenge. (As if I needed any more challenges dealing with housing insecurity at this time *and* my disability).

That morning, when Allan came to pick me up, I didn't want to go. But my mother looked at me and said, "Just try."

Alan drove us to La Jolla Cove, a small cove with a beach surrounded by cliffs in La Jolla, San Diego. My family and I had been to the beach there many times, but we always stuck to the cove or the shore. Open water? No, thank you! That was something I never imagined I would do. The pool was controlled; it had borders, railings to hold on to, many ways to get out. I knew how deep it was at all times, and there was always an edge I could get to and be safe. The ocean? The ocean was unpredictable and scary. I felt like one wrong move or a misplaced muscle would send me tumbling out into the Pacific. But Alan was certain I could do it.

Instead of us heading to the beach, Alan took me to the divers' access to the water. This access had four flights of stone stairs with a metal railing that led straight into the waves. No beach in sight. While surfers, drivers, and swimmers walked down the stairs to access the water, Alan had to carry me on his back. There was no handicap ramp, and there was no place to leave my prosthetics at the bottom. I guess they never imagined an amputee diving in here. (By the time I turned sixteen, I was strong enough to navigate the stairs by myself, putting one hand on the steps and bracing myself with the other on the metal railing.)

As we got closer to the bottom, the waves were licking the steps, and I couldn't see anything but the murky water. My fears crept back when I...

I think I see something in the water! Is it a shark? Oh my God, it's a shark!

"I don't think I can do it," I told Alan.

"I got you! It's just seaweed," he said, somehow reading my mind.

But I could think was, *I'm going to drown if I go in there.* I held onto Alan with a death grip as we got to the bottom step.

"I'm right here," he reassured me as he lowered me into the water, just as he'd done countless times at our practices at the pool. "Now swim out."

Swim out? He must be crazy!

I was freaking out, but I trusted him. I trusted him that day my mother brought me to the pool, and he watched me keep my distance while he worked with other children with disabilities. He didn't push me to get in. He just let me know that he was there. He had my back and I knew it.

"You *can* do this," Alan said.

I swam out just a few feet and quickly came back to the steps almost flailing my arms to get away from the seaweed "sharks." Alan gave me a few pointers: "Even out your stroke and round your shoulders," he said. I swam out a little farther and came back. Then a little bit farther and back. Alan was right there the whole time.

We did thirty minutes that day, but every practice session seemed to last an eternity. The anxiety and fear never left, but I didn't quit. I didn't want to disappoint Alan. He'd invested so much time in me, welcoming me to Challenged Athletes Foundation, when I was and helping me become such a strong swimmer in the years since. I wanted him to be proud. But the other part—probably the biggest part—was that I wanted to see what I could do. What could I *really* do if I kept going?

As I paddled in the open waters of the Pacific Ocean on the beautiful island of Kona, I marveled at how far I had come—from being petrified of being near the water at all to swimming more than two miles in a race with world-class athletes. *I* was a world-class athlete!

Focus. I steadied my breathing and looked for the next marker guiding the swimmers in a loop around a huge marina back to the shore.

Find the markers and keep moving forward.

Plunge and pull.

Strike, extend.

Pull and finish.

Strike, extend.

Pull and finish.

On the outside of my right shoulder, I managed to spot the three markers—they were red and white and the size of the sand-filled barrels they use at construction sites along the highway. They were hard to miss at this point.

Strike, extend.

Pull and finish.

I got closer and closer to the markers. After more than an hour in the water alone, I had caught up to the women's group on my way back to shore.

The sun was up over the horizon but not all the way out yet. As I passed one professional woman swimmer, I could finally see the docking area. *Yes*, I thought. I'd reached my goal. Finishing the race seemed all the more possible. *Now I just have to get to the shore.*

There was a giant Ironman balloon that became my target. I swam toward it with all of my strength. The entire beach had been converted into a transition area. Cheering crowds with bottles of water and Gatorade in hand were waiting for us to exit the water. There were tents with vendors and entertainment—bands and deejays, playing all kinds of music. There was even a section just for athletes with disabilities. Bikes lined the shoreline, and bags, shoes, and prosthetic legs littered the beach, all waiting for their owners to jump out of the ocean and into the next leg of the race. There was a changing area, which I didn't plan to use. Going there would eat up too much of my time. I would change on the beach.

As I approached the shore, the swells had grown, and the wind speed picked up. I was nauseous from the swells constantly swaying me up and down, back and forth. I had never been seasick before this day, so I was caught off guard by the feeling. But I pushed through. I couldn't let it slow me down.

I landed on the beach and literally crawled on all fours to the stairway out of the water. There were about eight steps to reach the boardwalk. Naturally, the Ironman volunteers were there and asked if I needed help or to be carried up. These are some of the nicest people I have ever encountered, so I politely declined. I was heavy, about a 150 pounds, even with my legs off. I knew it would take two people to carry me, especially while wet. Knowing that, I thought I would move faster by myself. I was used to carrying myself and I needed every bit of time.

I reached the platform, and Rudy was right there waiting for me with my running blades. Rudy Garcia-Tolson, a world-class five-time Paralympian and the first-ever above-the-knee amputee to finish an Ironman triathlon (finishing a race in Arizona; he had missed the cut at Kona in 2009). He was also one of my best friends, and he was there to make sure I became the first above-the-knee double amputee to finish this race.

I slid my legs on and headed to the physically challenged transition location. It had space for running legs, handcycles, racing wheelchairs, and daily wheelchairs. My team and I had set my food and equipment up the night before so I could easily access everything and get comfortable in my bike—a handcycle. It was about seven minutes before I took off on the next leg.

I had 112 miles of biking path waiting for me, and then a 26.2-mile run—a full marathon. Only then would I complete the Ironman Championship. Would I make history as the *first* above-knee double amputee to finish? That was between me and the stopwatch.

I knew one thing, however—no matter what time I finished, my mom would be waiting for me at the finish line.

Chapter Two

CRAWL BEFORE YOU WALK

A NURSE BROUGHT ME TO MY MOM IN THE RECOVERY ROOM tightly wrapped in a white blanket. The drama around my birth—my near death, the emergency C-section, all of the blood, and my dad fainting—had passed. Everything was clean and quiet. Even the volume on the TV was off, showing only the moving images of the aftermath of the riots.

My dad had gone off with his brother to celebrate. My mom was still groggy from the drugs. She would need almost two months to recover enough to return to work, but she couldn't wait to meet me.

The nurse had a pained look on her face when she handed me to my mom.

"What's wrong?" my mother questioned her.

"The doctor will be here shortly," was all she said as she placed my tightly swaddled body into my mom's arms, turned and left her alone with me. I guess she didn't want to be the one to tell my mother.

Mom smiled upon seeing my little dark chocolate face. She says I was a quiet baby and that seeing me for the first time filled her with joy. As she pulled back the blanket to inspect me, she immediately saw that there were some issues with my legs. The foot on my right leg was clubbed and had only four toes that weren't fully developed. I didn't have a foot on my left leg, just a lot of extra skin where the rest of the leg should have been. It looked as if a sock had been pulled down at the end and was left dangling and folded over.

My mother sat in her hospital bed holding me, she would later tell me. And she cried. She cried because I was alive. After six miscarriages, I made it. And I was beautiful. She also cried because she knew my life would be hard, much harder than she would have ever imagined or expected. Much harder than I deserved.

When the doctor who delivered me finally came to check on her, she didn't confront him or deliver a well-deserved, *I told you I saw something on the sonogram.* My mother had only one question.

"Will my baby ever walk?"

The doctor told her that it was unlikely. My tibias had not formed, so I would probably be a lifelong wheelchair user. "But he is healthy in every other way," the doctor said.

As my mother sat in her room holding me, there was a small television on the wall. Smoke from the riots in Los Angeles was still billowing across the screen. It seemed as if the whole city was engulfed in smoke and the entire nation was watching.

My baby will never walk? she thought. *What kind of life will my son have?*

I was a dark-skinned African American male—a struggle in itself in the United States. *And* I would be physically disabled? Mom took a deep breath. She dried her tears and did what she has done most of her life. She pushed through. There was no time for pity. She had a child to raise. And she would soon find out she was going to be doing it by herself.

My father didn't leave immediately or all at once. He was simply not there. Was my disability the reason my father did not stick around? I'll never know. But I do believe he was just too immature at the time to be a father to anyone. He was starting to "hang out" a lot and not come home at night. My mother suspected he was with other women. And he wasn't carrying his weight in terms of bills—constantly in and out of jobs. My disability was just one more excuse for him to take off, I guess.

A year after I was born, my father had already gotten three more women pregnant. He had three more babies! Still, my mother never said a bad word about my dad. She did her best to include him in raising me. When I was old enough to talk, she made sure I spoke to him on the phone. She kept pictures of him around the house. I just thought Daddy was off somewhere working. And I was fine with it. I didn't miss him.

I had plenty of family—my aunts and cousins and my grandma. Later, my dad's family, my uncle and my other grandmother, came into the picture. I didn't want for attention or love, though mom herself was raised on tough love. She was the oldest of eleven—all girls, with two who died in childhood. So she was changing diapers, feeding babies, washing clothes, and babysitting most of her childhood.

"I can't remember a year when Mama wasn't pregnant," she says. "All I know about is taking care of babies! It's one of the reasons why I waited so long to have a baby of my own. I never really wanted to have a child until I met your dad."

My mom was thirty when she got pregnant for the first time. Just about all of her sisters had children by then, and she was enjoying being an auntie. After the third, then fourth, then fifth miscarriage, she didn't know if she could become a mom. The sixth time she lost her baby, she had given up hope. Then, shortly afterward, she was pregnant with me.

So as she lay in the hospital bed, afraid but determined with me in her arms, she couldn't wait to introduce me to the family. The hospital workers sent her home after a week, still raw from the C-section with no instructions on how to care for me.

"I understood diaper changing and feeding and all of that. But I had no idea how to care for your legs."

Fortunately, one of her sisters worked in the health-care field as a nurse. My aunt helped my mom through it all.

"Marian, you have to keep the folds around his legs clean and dry or he could get a rash or even an infection," she told her. She described it the way you clean around foreskin of an uncircumcised penis. "If you don't clean that area good, it will also stink."

My mother was back to work within eight weeks of giving birth, since maternity leave would not be enacted into law in the country until the next year. Her job gave her two extra weeks off because of the complicated birth, but the two extra weeks were unpaid, which is still the case in states that don't offer paid parental leave. If not for the baby shower her friends and family threw, I might not have had diapers. My medical expenses weren't covered by her insurance, either. So she was back to work. The Department of Defense transferred her to a different department. No more forklifts to operate and fifty-pound boxes to throw, but she was still the only woman in this new section. There was no ladies room, and she needed to pump her breasts at least once while at work. Out of options, she used one of the men's rooms on the far end of her floor.

"It was pretty disgusting. I cleaned one stall and sat there during my lunch break and pumped my breast. I would hear men coming in and out while I was there, but I had to do what I had to do."

While my mom worked and struggled to make ends meet at her still-demanding job, I stayed with my aunt, the nurse, who had a house closer to my mom's job on the west side of San Diego. She had two children, both older than me. By the time I was eight or nine months old, I was staying with my grandmother while mom worked.

My mom found a little two-bedroom wood frame house, with a view of the canyon out back. It had a big yard. And at the back of our little yellow house, the first house I remember living in, was a bigger house with an even better view of the canyon. My grandmother moved into that house. Every day, my mom would leave for work, walking out our backdoor down ten steep steps to the walkway leading to my grandmother's front door.

My grandma's house is where I discovered my limits—or lack thereof. I was active in the womb, but outside of it, I was unstoppable.

Grandma's house was the hub—full of kids, mostly her own grandchildren, but also kids from the neighborhood who stayed there while their parents worked. My grandmother was a tough woman. Some may have considered her mean—she definitely was not someone to play with or play pranks on. All my cousins were scared of Grandma, but she adored me. She really doted on me, but she didn't baby me or treat me as if I was disabled or different. I did get privileges though—mainly not getting whooped for small and major infractions the way my cousins did.

Grandma set up a playpen in her living room for me so that I wouldn't get trampled by the other children, but I soon discovered my superpower—I could climb. I didn't have working legs, but my arms more than made up for that. At around eight months, I started climbing out of my playpen, and soon enough, I was climbing onto furniture and getting around the house. By two, I was so good at using my hands and arms that I was keeping up with my cousins in games of tag and wrestling matches. I also started "crawling" earlier than expected. Really, I was dragging myself around by my arms because the folds of skin around my limbs and the undeveloped foot would get caught under my thighs and I had to rock back and forth to release the loose skin, lift myself up, and get moving again. I often had to stop when the shock of pain would shoot through my limbs. I would cry from the pain and also the frustration because I couldn't move.

"You can hear the gristle in your legs popping. You would whimper and whine, but you never stopped," my mother observed. "That extra skin was slowing you down." That's when my mom had to make a decision. Was it time to think about getting me a wheelchair? Or, perhaps, look at removing the foot and leg altogether?

At this point, my mom's life was filled with doctor's appointments and work. She was working ten- to twelve-hour shifts at least three to four times a month so that she could take off days to shuttle me to and from the pediatrician. She consulted quite a few doctors regarding my legs. Most of them gave her the same two choices. Option 1: leave the legs as they were. Sure, they stopped me from moving at times, but I was growing stronger and able to use my arms to get around pretty well. I would eventually need a wheelchair and would likely be confined to it the rest of my life.

Option 2: remove the legs.

Option 2 meant that my legs would be amputated above the knee. I may still need to use a wheelchair, several doctors warned. But with an amputation, there was a strong possibility that I could learn to walk with the help of prosthetics. Option 2 was expensive. Prosthetics were deemed durable medical equipment. They cost thousands of dollars, and they were not covered by mom's insurance.

My mom had saved about $30,000 by that time. We had a home. We had a car. But if she chose option 2, that money would be gone quickly. Not only would the surgeries and the rehab be expensive, but as I grew, I would need new prosthetics. If she chose option 1, which her mom and a couple of her sisters wanted her to do, she knew I would need to use a wheelchair for the rest of my life and be in a lot of pain. *Not an option*, she thought.

She wanted to explore every *other* option before making this life-altering decision for me. She consulted with several doctors and even visited the Shriners Hospital for Children to see how children with my kind of disability were managing. The hospital opened in the 1920s to treat children affected by polio, which, among other symptoms, could leave someone in so much pain they couldn't walk. President Franklin D. Roosevelt was a wheelchair user because he was stricken with polio as a child. Today, Shriner's Hospital helps children all over the country—especially children like me. My mom thought the doctors there could give her some clear guidance. She found a location in San Diego, took off work, and we went to meet children who would be wheelchair users forever. There were children with everything from severe scoliosis and spina bifida to cerebral palsy and paralysis from a spinal cord injury.

She saw four or five more doctors at different hospitals and facilities after that—all gave her a lot to think about. One doctor even suggested waiting until I was eighteen years old so that I could make this decision myself. She consulted the family, too. Half of her sisters said she should have my legs amputated. The other half said, "Keep them!" My grandmother was firmly in the "keep them" camp.

"He's getting around fine," she said. "Leave them the way they are. Why put him through all of that? He's fine."

Grandma was right. I was getting around well. I could pull myself up and climb. I would fall a lot, too. But I never cried when I fell. I would just get back up and climb again. At the same time, my mother saw my frustration when the extra skin would roll under my legs. I would be reaching for my bottle or trying to race the other kids, and the folds would get caught under me. And because I was so active, lint and dirt and stuff would get caught up in the folds. My mom was tempted to just pick me up, but she also never wanted to baby me. She knew I needed to find my independence. She would get on my grandmother's case, too, who would sometimes try to carry me when she saw me struggling.

"What's he going to do when we aren't around one day?" my mother would say to Grandma. "He's going to have to fend for himself. He's going to have to figure it out."

It broke Mom's heart every time I got stuck and started to whimper. She could see how much I wanted to go but couldn't. So she decided to take the brakes off. She followed the advice of the doctor who suggested immediate amputation above the knee.

"He will be walking in no time," the doctor assured her. He also suggested that they start fitting me for prosthetics as soon as I healed.

That's what she needed to hear.

My mother never talked to me as if I was a baby, cooing in a high pitch or goo-goo gah-ing. She would talk to me as if she were talking to one of her siblings or any adult. Before I went in to have the surgery, she gathered me onto her lap on our couch and told me what was going to happen.

"You won't have your legs slowing you down anymore," she told me. "Remember that movie we watched with the pirate?"

My mom loved watching old movies. Later, it would become one of our things—getting a bunch of movies and spending the weekend watching them and binging on popcorn.

"You saw how the pirate was able to walk on his peg leg?" she said. "Well, one day, you will be able to walk, too. Don't you want to walk?"

She later told me that after seeing how well I was getting around before the amputation, she could imagine what an upgrade the prosthetics would be. She knew I would master them, too. And she also thought it was just a matter of time before they came up with some futuristic version of the peg leg. Heck, they may even have a bionic leg one day. Little did she know . . .

She scheduled my amputation—both legs, above the knee. I was two years old. I don't remember the operation, but I do remember the recovery. I remember the long hospital stay. I remember the bandages that had to be changed frequently and the kindness of the nurses, who were so different from the stern, cold doctors. And I remember the pain.

After I was discharged, my mother didn't have many options for childcare. She couldn't afford to take any more time off work. While Grandma's house was convenient, my mother didn't want me to stay there. There were too many children, for one. Grandma would barely keep up with them, let alone a child recovering from a double leg amputation. And the house wasn't the cleanest either.

I didn't notice, nor did I care. All I remember is that Grandma's house was fun! The very thing my mom was nervous about—too many kids—I loved! Grandma had a huge den full of toys. It was like an indoor playground. There was an Easy-Bake Oven for my cousin Brittney and dolls for the other girls. There were action figures for the boys. There was even a plastic teeter-totter in the middle of the room. Before my surgery, I spent a lot of time on that thing. My cousin Dwanye would try to flip me in the air by jumping on the other side really hard. Without legs, I didn't weigh a whole lot, so staying on my side was a challenge. But I held my own. I never let him propel me in the air the way he wanted. I just remember holding on to the handle for dear life. We were rowdy, rough, and doing the most. Every day was an adventure.

My grandmother mostly hung out in her room playing music on her old record player...loud! While we played, she would rotate her soul, blues, and jazz albums. We always knew when one of her favorite songs was playing because she would let out a "whooooo!" and then we'd hear her clapping and tapping her foot to the beat. Booker T & the MG's "Green Onion" was her number one. She kept that song on repeat.

After my surgery, she tried to keep me in the playpen for safety, but as soon as I could, I was climbing out to play. One day, I was in the living room playing with action figures by myself. It was rare to be alone in that house with so many kids coming through and leaving out. Alongside the cousins, some kids came to her house after kindergarten or preschool, which was still a year or two away for me. One of these kids, who must have just gotten out of kindergarten, saw me playing and came into the den. He had to be four years old or so and was a whole lot bigger than me. When I saw him, I was happy because I would have someone to play with. But before that thought finished in my head, he walked over and stomped on my bandaged stumps. I remember the tan Timberlands to this day, big and clunky for a kid even as big as him. I let out an ear-splitting scream that had my grandma running into the room. I never cried, so she knew something was truly wrong. The force of his giant shoe busted my stitches, which had not yet been removed after my surgery. All I remember were those boots, the pain, and the blood.

My grandmother started hollering too after seeing the blood. She rushed me to the hospital, where they stitched me back up and sent me home. Thankfully, there wasn't any structural damage to my legs.

When my mother came to pick me up from Grandma's, she was beyond angry with my grandmother. Their relationship was off and on during my mom's adult life, so it didn't take much for my mother to keep her distance from her mother. And my injury became a big deal.

"Why weren't you watching him!" my mother yelled. "Where were you when this happened?!"

"Don't you talk to me like that," Grandma said. She was not someone who allowed disrespect, even if she was wrong. Grandma was tough. But when it came to me, my mother was tougher. My mother held a lot of resentment toward her mother from childhood. It was always bubbling at the surface. My birth seemed to melt away some of the iciness between them. But this incident brought it all back.

The incident sent my mother scrambling to figure out what to do with me. Leaving me to stay with my grandmother while she worked was convenient and cost effective but not her ideal choice, even before I got hurt. The busted stitches meant she had to take off from work again. All the while, the medical bills from this most recent visit were piling up on top of the bills from the amputation.

It seemed as if there was an endless flow of medical expenses. And her health care didn't cover them all.

She stayed home as long as she could with me before giving in and sending me back to my grandmother's house.

My mom was apprehensive about me going back. But she didn't have a choice. I was also scared to go back to Grandma's after what happened, even after my stumps were fully healed. My mother could tell I wasn't totally on board with going back. So she sat me down to have a talk before dropping me off. I was three years old, but my mother always talked to me like I had sense.

"You're going back to your Grandma's," she told me. "If anybody bothers you, you ball up your fist and you hit them as hard as you can. Don't let *anyone* stomp on your legs or hurt you again!" She said that last part with force.

The first couple of days back at my grandma's were like old times. I didn't see the boy and I played happily with no incidents. But on the third day, there he was, the same boy, wearing those same Timberland boots. And there I was again, playing in the living room by myself. It was déjà vu.

Inside I was petrified, thinking about what my mother told me to do. I didn't want to hit anybody, but I also didn't want him to hurt me again. When he got close, I didn't give him a chance to speak or do anything, I balled up my little fist and pulled it behind me like I was winding up to pitch a baseball. When he leaned down over me where I was sitting, I swung upwards with all my might. I connected with the side of his face. *Wham!*

When I think back, he probably was coming in peace to apologize.

But all I could think of was the pain he caused me the last time and nothing else. When my fist connected, I saw the confusion and the pain and *fear* in his eyes. He let out a yell, followed by a rush of tears.

In an instant, the tables turned. And I didn't like the feeling of making him cry. Plus my little fist hurt. I felt terrible, but he never bothered me again. My mom's advice worked! I learned that you have to confront your fears (something I'd have to work through a few more times before I mastered it), but also that sometimes things are not how they appear. I also learned that bullies are cowards.

And just like that, Grandma's house was the fun house again.

A few weeks after I got my stitches out, I was up to my old tricks. My stumps were still tender, but I could put weight on them, which was very unusual for above-the-knee amputees. For many, "standing" on their stumps is quite painful. But I could stand on mine. I would hold on to the edge of the couch or a table and see how long I could stand.

Soon, the tenderness went away, and I took my first steps ever. There were a bunch of kids playing in the living room when I grabbed the edge of my grandmother's coffee table and pulled myself up. I let go, stepped forward, and plopped onto my backside. My cousin Debbie saw me and egged me on.

"You got this, Roderick!"

I pulled myself back up and took a couple of more steps before falling backward on my behind again.

"Do it again!" said Debbie. I did. By the end of the day, I could walk a few steps on my stumps. More importantly, I was *confident*.

Soon, I was able to even jump and land on my stumps. I could climb up on the furniture and jump down onto the carpet. My grandmother had a plush, red shag carpet in her den, so the land-ing was soft. I did this with reckless abandon and total joy. I dis-covered, however, that I needed to stick to soft surfaces for my landings. One afternoon, I climbed up on my grandmother's kitchen counter, which was more than three feet off the ground, for some cereal. I got the box of Cap'n Crunch from the cabinet and jumped down from the counter. The jolt of pain that shot through my stumps made me instantly drop the box of cereal and grab the bottom of my stumps. The pain was searing enough for me to never try that again. Oh, I definitely climbed back up onto the counter a couple of days after I recovered. But from then on, I slowly and carefully *climbed* back to the floor. No more jumping onto linoleum or other hard surfaces for me.

My grandmother, who was dead set against my legs being amputated, was a silent cheerleader of my progress. She wasn't someone who showed a ton of affection, but I knew she was in my corner by what she *didn't* do or say. While my cousins were con-stantly yelled at—"Dwanye, sit your behind down somewhere!" or "Brittney, get off that couch before I whoop you!"—with me, there were no limits. She never told me that I couldn't do something. She saw me walking and climbing, and she never once told me to get off her furniture. That was love!

———

By the time I was getting comfortable with my disability at home, our lives were changing again. My mother sat me down to tell me we had to move. My mom's job was demanding, but she wasn't making enough money to keep up with the bills. She had taken off a lot of time for my doctor's visits. No work, no pay, which meant we would often fall short of even the basics—food, electricity, and gas for the car.

So, Mom did what she knew how to do: research and come up with a plan. She found out that if we were on government assistance, *all* my medical costs would be covered—including the prosthetics that I would need as I grew older. The catch: to get this aid, we needed to qualify. We didn't have much as it was, but we did have a house, a car, and savings. My mother had managed to save $30,000 before my amputation. And her salary was way over the monthly maximum to qualify. With our debt and monthly expenses, my mother was running in the negative each month. She knew she could not keep it going.

I was going on four years old, but I do remember around this time my mom becoming irritable. She always made an effort to sing to me in the mornings before we left the house, and she always seemed to find laughter. Her laugh was contagious. But in the stress of moving and considering our future, her laughter was becoming rare.

She became shorter with me than usual. I remember one night, I climbed onto the cabinet to get something, and I knocked over a glass and broke it. She yelled at me, something she almost never did. Not long after, I heard her crying in her room for the very first time. I didn't know how to respond. I felt bad for breaking the glass and making my mother cry. But she wasn't crying over a broken glass. She was crying over a broken life. She must have been tormented during those last days before she made the ultimate sacrifice. After an hour or so, she was back to herself. She came and hugged me and told me everything would be alright. She tucked me in, kissed me on my forehead, and went back to her room.

I was three and I had my own room. My mother believed it was important that I sleep in my own room and get used to being independent, even at that young age. It's funny how I took having my own room for granted. Like it was a given.

Over the next year, our living situation slowly declined, and my mother's emotions did too. She would have bad days, with outbursts of anger, followed by tears. Those bad days were becoming more and more frequent.

Things started to change. The first major change was moving from our little yellow house behind Grandma's. My grandmother moved first to the other side of San Diego into an apartment complex. She said she was tired of taking care of children. Of course, her new two-bedroom apartment was also filled with children. Her new complex had a swimming pool. In the summer, my cousins spent most days splashing and playing. They loved to swim, but I was terrified of the water. So that summer, I was content being in the apartment with Grandma.

Then, my mom found an apartment close by for her and me to live in. This was our first apartment, a one-bedroom nearby so that I could still stay with Grandma during the day to maintain a sense of normalcy. In the summers, I would also be at my aunt Myra's. Between Grandma's and Aunt Myra's house, I gained a lot of confidence and independence, which would come in handy because I would be starting school—regular school with abled children—in the fall.

With my cousins, I wasn't the boy without legs. I was Roderick, who was just as tough as the rest of them. I felt normal in my family. But soon I would have to go to school. And that meant I had to overcome another fear—walking with prosthetics.

Chapter Three

WALK

"Look what we have here, Roderick Sewell," Mama sang out. I was in my room at home playing with a Teenage Mutant Ninja Turtle action figure. I loved them. My favorite? It was a tie between the leader Leonardo in blue, which was my favorite color at the time, and Donatello, the genius in purple.

Hearing her call to me, I was suspicious because when my mother used my full name—"Roderick Sewell!"—it usually meant something was up.

I stopped what I was doing and "walked" into the living room on my hands. She was on the couch with a bag sitting next to her.

"Come see what I have for you," she said smiling. She presented this bag like it was a Christmas or birthday gift. From inside, she pulled out a pair of tiny legs. These little brown legs looked like they were made of wood or hard plastic. My mom sat me on her lap and attached the legs to my stumps. They had a rubber band where the knee would be so they looked like the legs you might see on a marionette, like Pinocchio's legs. There were also straps that went around my waist to hold them in place. They were uncomfortable and didn't fit well at all. And I needed to use a walker to walk with them. For the first time in my life, I felt restricted.

"Let's see you take a step," Mama said as she lowered me from the couch.

My mother tried to get me to walk on these new, wobbly legs. I had gotten pretty good walking on my stumps. These legs felt strange. I couldn't move the way I was used to, and they were too complicated to take on and off. I didn't want them.

"Don't you want to be a big boy?" my mother said, watching my hesitancy. I looked down at these weird brown, strange things awkwardly attached to my stumps, and I was angry and confused. I started to cry. *Why was she making me do this?*

My mother, seeing this, took the legs off and put them back in the bag. She laid the bag down next to me, and I nudged it away with my stumps. I didn't want any parts of the bag or what was in it.

I was still three years old. I wasn't a big boy. And I didn't want to wear these legs. So my mother didn't force the issue. Not then.

A year later, she was back with new legs. This time, she wasn't taking no for an answer. One of the requirements for starting school was that I had to have prosthetics. It was a hazard for me to walk around the building on my hands, even though I was used to it. My cousins and friends at Aunt Myra's and Grandma's knew how to be careful around me while still having fun; my classmates wouldn't. I had to go to school, and I had to use these legs.

These new ones looked better than the ones from before. They had upgraded the rubber band to a mechanical knee with a carbon-fiber socket. There was no waist belt, and I didn't need a walker. These legs were colorful and playful. Each part was a different color. They were cool. But I still didn't want them!

My mother talked to me a lot about getting ready for school. I was headed to preschool in the fall with all the other kids. She put the legs on me and stood me in front of the mirror.

"You need to get comfortable with these so that you can go to school, Roderick Sewell," she said.

I looked at myself in the mirror, and I started crying. I looked at her, and she looked as if she wanted to cry too. But I also saw that she wasn't going to give in. She had a stern stare with watery eyes, and I realized this was serious. My mother never cried. She couldn't let me take these off. I couldn't put this off for another month, let alone one year. I rocked on those legs and became determined to get comfortable.

I never thought about *not* having legs until that very moment. In my entire four years on earth, I was never made to feel that something was "wrong" with me. I mean, of course, everyone around me was taller than me—even the babies. But I never thought of myself as disabled or different. I have to thank my family for that. They treated me like everyone else—except for my grandmother, Freddie Mae Jackson, who gave me *extra* love and grace.

The prosthetics would set me apart. Make me different from everyone else at school.

I didn't know anyone else that had them. In the legs, I wasn't as nimble. I wasn't as graceful. I wasn't fast. I fell the first few times I tried to even stand up in them. I had fallen before, but with the prosthetics, the falls were unpredictable and awkward. Without them, I could climb and walk on my hands. With them, I stood out in a different way.

I cried, but the tears didn't work as they had the year before.

The next day, Mama helped me put those legs on again. I cried again. She ignored my tears. "Just one step, baby. You can do it."

Every day, this was our routine. She would put on the legs, and I would cry. She would encourage me to take one step, just one. She even tried to bribe me. But there wasn't a chocolate chip cookie on Earth that could make me *want* to walk with those legs. I did try, though. I tried because she asked me to. I always tried for my mom. It's as if I knew she was struggling, and I didn't want to be one more thing she had to fight.

I let her put on the legs, and I gave walking a shot again. I'd get a couple of steps in, and knee joints would buckle, and I would fall. It reminded me of learning how to walk on my stumps, holding on to my grandma's furniture. I took a few steps and fell. I cried. I took a couple more steps and fell again. And cried. My mother wouldn't let me quit. So, I kept going. Eventually, I was walking without having to hold her hand. It wasn't comfortable. I looked like a soldier in the *March of the Wooden Soldiers*. But like it or not, I was walking.

What I didn't know was that my mother had sacrificed everything for me to have these prosthetics. Knowing that I would need new ones as I grew and her insurance didn't cover them or my future care, she made a decision that would alter our lives. I didn't know that these would be the last couple of years in our own place with our own car.

I didn't know what was coming.

———

My mom was giddy as she dressed me in a crisp white shirt, a black sweater, and black shorts. It was the first day of preschool at Johnson Magnet School in Emerald Hills. I was fidgety and nervous before leaving the house. I was uncomfortable, maybe even a little scared, and not just because I knew I'd have to wear the prosthetic legs. I wasn't used to being around a lot of strangers. I knew my cousin Brittney would be there. She was in the first grade; her class would be right down the hall from mine. Still, this would be the first time outside of my comfort zone.

For the first four years of my life, I'd been in a bubble, surrounded by people who loved me. They didn't treat me like a boy with a disability. I was just Roderick, one of the cousins who liked to play rough and could hold his own in a game of tag.

I didn't know what to expect at school. I got a glimpse of what people outside of my loving family were like when Mom and I went shopping. I would notice people staring at me in the store, but I didn't have to make friends with those people or see them every day. Were the kids in my class going to stare at me, too?

My mother saw my face, and she could sense I was nervous.

She kneeled down in front of me, so I was at eye level, and said, "You're going to school with the other big boys and girls. And you're going to have fun!"

I wasn't convinced.

"It's going to be a great day!" my mom sang, trying to hype me up. She had a way of smiling and finding laughter in any situation. She took out her camera and started taking a bunch of pictures, but I still wasn't really a happy camper.

We had breakfast and headed out to pick up Brittney, who lived closer to Johnson Magnet School. When we arrived at the campus, my mom parked the car and helped me put on my legs. She held my hand as the three of us walked toward the school.

"Wait, Roderick," she said and turned with that camera. "Smile!"

I didn't smile.

My mom had me pose in front of the school, inside the school, and even when I got into the classroom. We dropped Brittney off at her class on the second floor and then paused when we got downstairs for more pictures.

I get it. My mom had spent weeks preparing me for this day. Hours and days of walking and falling, and learning how to start, stop, and pivot. I mastered my prosthetics, which was mandatory for me to attend school. We practiced walking into the classroom the first day. She told me about the playground and all the equipment I could expect there. She reminded me not to roughhouse and not to let anyone mess with me. We even practiced going to the bathroom, which we both knew would be a chore. My mother taught me early on how to climb up on the toilet and do my business. She taught me how to go from the toilet to the sink to wash my hands. That was in our home, which was clean. In public, I couldn't do that. I had to practice going while standing up in my prosthetics for number 1. But what if I had to go number 2?

I couldn't do that wearing my prosthetics, so my mom arranged with the school for me to use the bathroom in the nurse's office for that. She had it all worked out.

But *I* didn't have it all worked out. My mom walked with me to my classroom. The teacher was there smiling, holding open the classroom door. I could see all of the desks and the children. My mom let go of my hand and told said, "Have a good day, baby!'

I wanted to cry as I watched my mom leave. But I didn't want to seem like a baby. I entered the classroom. The room was bright and full of cartoon characters and numbers and letters lining the walls. Each desk had a coloring book and crayons.

I could hear a few whispers as I made my way to an empty desk at the back of the room.

"What's wrong with him?"

"He's weird!"

And the stares. So many eyes were glued to me. Some were curious; others seemed interested. Some still looked mad. It was worse than the grocery store stares because my mom and I didn't stay in the grocery store all day. I was trapped in this room with these stares for hours.

When recess finally came, the teacher led us to the playground. I was standing there alone when a boy named Brandon came up to me and asked me if I wanted to play.

"Do you wanna go on the jungle gym?" he asked.

I had no idea what a jungle gym was, but when I walked up to the big metal dome made of connected triangles, I knew I could climb it. I was used to playing with other children—thanks to spending so much time at my grandma's house and Aunt Myra's house—but the slides and the swings and the jungle gym were all new to me. I was still adventurous and pretty curious, so I kicked off my prosthetics and started my way up the jungle gym. I beat Brandon to the top and we sat there for a minute and talked. Brandon and I became friends that day. A few other kids came to play with us—three girls. That became my crew throughout my time at Johnson Magnet School. That day, we played with blocks in the sandbox, and I even tried the swing for the first time.

I was able to get into the swing, holding on to the chains and hoisting myself onto the seat. But I couldn't figure out how to make it go back and forth. Swings require you to swing your legs to get lift, so I mainly swayed slowly, side to side. (My mother would later take me to a park in our neighborhood to show me how to use the swing with my disability. "You have to really put your hips into it," she'd tell me.)

By the end of the week, I started to look forward to school. I liked the routine. I liked the teacher. I now had a couple of friends, and I loved learning. I liked story time, and of course, I loved playing during recess. It took about a week for the stares to stop, and I discovered that children really don't care much about differences. After the initial shock of seeing me wore off, I was just like the rest of them.

I learned early how to fit in and to know that, while I had limitations, they were always worth pushing past. I took these lessons home with me. Some of my best memories as a child involved doing things that seemed impossible—like walking in my prosthetics and, later, swimming. Summertime was family time. Cookouts, beach, Aunt Myra's. The cookouts were at her house because she had the biggest yard.

We played until the sun went down. I loved playing tag. Somehow, I managed to keep up and even catch my cousins while "running" on my hands and stumps. I still preferred not to use my prosthetics at home, so when I discovered the Tupperware cups, it was on. My cousins had scooters and bikes and skateboards, which were exciting to me. And with those cups suctioned onto my stumps, I could run around the yard with the best of them!

"Can I sit on it?" I asked one of them about their skateboard. At first, I wasn't going anywhere, just sitting on it. I could only go side to side, much like the swings on the playground, or zoom forward a short distance when someone pushed the board while I was on it. Gradually, though, I started to figure it out. If I put the Tupperware cups on my stumps, I could push off the ground with them and then use my hands to propel me forward. That took me around in circles. Eventually, after a few rounds of *let me try this out* and *I wonder what I can do*, I was off to the races. Now the trick was how to stop! I used my hands, and, in the beginning, I would run over my fingers or scrape up my palms on the pavement. I borrowed Aunt Myra's gardening gloves, and that solved that problem.

I even learned to drive a motorized toy truck, thanks to Uncle Joseph. As my cousins were zipping around the yard on their Big Wheels and tricycles, Uncle Joseph made me a motorized toy truck that I could propel using my hip. He was some kind of engineer, and he moved the truck's pedal so that instead of needing a foot to engage the motor, I could press against the pedal with my butt and take off.

In addition to being a great engineer, Uncle Joseph also manned the grill and was responsible for feeding us hot dogs and hamburgers. He wasn't a blood uncle. The rumor was he dated one of my aunts (I still don't know which one), and when they broke up, he never left the family. In a family full of women, he was one of the first positive male figures in my life. He was always looking out for me and making me laugh.

My life was filled with people who loved me and looked out for me, and now classmates who were beginning to accept me. And I kept adding new people, too. My grandmother finally got approved for Section 8 housing and moved into a nice, but much smaller, apartment across town, leaving my mom without convenient childcare. Then came Miss Pope. She was an older Black woman my mom met at my school. She had a couple of grandchildren she would drop off and pick up, and she ran a daycare out of her home a couple of blocks from Johnson Elementary. Meeting her was perfect timing, since my mother didn't have a place for me to go after school.

"I have room for him!" Miss Pope said. She took a liking to me. She used to call me "boyfriend." "Boyfriend, how was your day today?" she would say. "Boyfriend, would you like some hotdogs?"

Miss Pope was an older lady but very agile and active, keeping up with the seven or eight children under the age of ten who stayed with her until their parents picked them up. I loved going to her house because, for one, she treated me well. She loved my complexion, which she would comment on frequently. She was also an inspirational Black woman who knew a lot of history, so she very wise. She wasn't just a babysitter or daycare owner; she made sure we had books, and she talked to us about things to build our character.

"You are all are smart and important," she would tell us. "Don't ever let anyone tell you different!"

A lot of the kids from school would be there, too. I was building my village.

I had cousins and the kids in the neighborhood on the weekend. I had my afterschool crew at Miss Pope's. I had my in-school school crew—Brandon, Pearl, Reyanna, Ambrosia, and Mikayla—during the day.

I was enjoying school—learning spelling and English pretty quickly. We had a piano in our classroom, and each morning, our teacher, Mr. Callahan, would play us a song to start the day. None of us could sing very well, but it was fun trying.

I had friends. I had a sense of belonging and normalcy. I was finally fitting in.

At home, things were starting to change.

Chapter Four

MARIAN'S STORY

WHILE MY MOTHER WAS MAKING SURE I COULD STAND ON MY own, she was still wading through issues of her own that kept knocking her off balance. My mother made a decision that at the time made sense. She decided to sacrifice everything—our home, car, and life as we knew it—so that I could have a chance at a future. What she did sounded unwise—isn't a roof over our heads and reliable transportation more important than prosthetics? Who would do something like that, especially with a child with my disability? And I must admit, there were several times while we were moving from shelter to shelter, from San Diego to Alabama, when I, too, wondered, *Why?* Why did we have to live this way?

But I never questioned my mother's love for me. Or her commitment to doing the best she could for me.

And I never challenged her (not until I was almost an adult).

I chose to walk in her shoes and see things through her lens. I chose to understand.

———

The county truant officer pulled up to my grandparents' railroad shack. It was one of a dozen that sat on the outskirts of the strawberry fields, tomato patches, and orange groves. There was a dirt road leading to the itinerant farm "village," which housed migrant farmers from Spanish-speaking countries and a couple of Black families, like mine. It was in the middle of nowhere, Florida. But the truant officer found them.

My grandfather, who during this season was one of many hands picking strawberries, was out in the fields. My grandmother was in the yard, a baby on one knee, one in her belly, snapping peas into a bowl. The truant officer pulled up, kicking up dust, put the car in park, got out, and walked over to my grandmother.

"Good morning, Ma'am," he said. "I am looking for Marian. She hasn't been to school in a couple of months, and I wanted to make sure she was okay. Is everything okay?"

"She's fine," Grandma said.

My mother was nine years old and hadn't been to school all year. The administration reported her missing. When the officer asked my grandmother why she hadn't showed up to the fourth grade, my grandmother answered simply, "She's needed here!"

My grandfather drove the bus that transported the laborers to the different farms where they picked mostly beans and tomatoes. This was in Homestead, Florida.

My grandmother was pregnant with her seventh child (my aunt Freddy Jane) in nine years. There were Martha, Milton, Melody, Myra, and my mother, Marian, the firstborn, named after her grandmothers, both of whom were named Mary.

As the oldest sibling, my nine-year-old mom, was pressed into service—cleaning the house, babysitting, feeding the babies, changing the babies, and washing the diapers. There were no single-use Pampers back then, and if they did have Pampers, that was a luxury my mother's family couldn't afford. They had cloth diapers, or any old rag that could be attached to the babies with a safety pin. And when they ran out of safety pins, my mother had to get creative with string or rubber bands.

My mother would have to wash out the cloth diapers and hang them on a line to dry. As long as Mama can remember, she was taking care of the house and babies. Practically her entire childhood, there were at least two babies in diapers at a time. She learned how to cook as soon as she was old enough to stand on a chair and tend to the pots.

"I would get a chair and stand over the stove because I was too small to reach," she told me. "The first thing I learned to cook was eggs...when we could get them...and fried baloney, and hoecakes for breakfast. I knew how to make that real good. I made that stretch for the older kids, while the babies got Carnation or PET milk."

On some days when she was needed, my grandfather would have her in the field working with him. Extra bushels meant extra money, which was sorely needed for the extra mouths that seemed to come every year. Each year, my grandfather would pack up the family to head to the next farm that may pay a couple of cents more per bushel. The work was seasonal, so they would move where the work and the money were.

The family spent most of their time on farms and farming community in Homestead, right outside of Miami. To be so close to the hustle and bustle of the city and the beach of what they called the Sunshine State was almost cruel. My mother's childhood had very little joy.

School was one of the few places where she thrived. She loved reading and learning, but even that was being taken from her. She had hoped when that truant officer showed up that day, he would make my grandmother send her back. But when she barked at him, "I need her here!" he looked at the situation, got back in his car, and drove away.

My mother remembers being sad. She also remembers the work of trying to keep a house with all those children. It was overwhelming for everyone.

"The house was always dirty," my mother told me.

There was no indoor plumbing. Keeping up with the diapers was one thing, but keeping the clothes clean was nearly impossible. She shared a bed with four siblings.

"And every night someone would piss in the bed!" she remembers. "We were just smelling like piss all of the time."

While she had loved school in the third grade, it was also a source of embarrassment because she was often sent to school smelly. "Yes, I was made fun of," she remembers.

But at least she got to read and learn. She would have taken the unkind words over what she had waiting for her back at home. At age nine, my mother made up her mind that she didn't want to have children. She had had enough of diapers and crying babies to last her a lifetime. And if she wanted to enjoy a baby, all she had to do was go to her mother's house.

"I had enough with babies growing up," she told me. "But then I met your dad."

He was handsome, smooth-talking, a ladies' man. And he swept my mother off her feet. She was in her thirties and not thinking about settling down. But she got pregnant, and everything changed. She had a miscarriage pretty early on in their relationship. But something was awakened in her.

"I was heartbroken after losing my first baby," she later told me. "I honestly, didn't believe I could get pregnant. But I cannot describe the feeling of that little life growing inside me. I wanted that feeling. I wanted a baby. I wanted *my* baby!"

Perhaps for the first time, she could imagine the perfect family. She could have a home of her own, a husband, and a couple of children. She could see it. She allowed herself to dream.

A couple of more miscarriages came quickly back to back. Then came the rumors of my father fooling with other women. Then she discovered she was pregnant again, with me.

She put aside the dream of the perfect life and had one focus— the baby that was growing inside of her.

"Just let me have this baby. Let *this* baby live! I will do anything for this child!"

I don't know that anyone ever truly loved my mother—not

even my father. At least I don't believe she has ever felt or known true love. She didn't feel it from her mother and father. She didn't feel it from my father. And yet she had so much love for me.

Somehow, she managed to find love for me. She wanted to make sure I had the love she never did.

She sacrificed. She sacrificed everything for me.

Chapter Five

THE HOUSE WAS THE FIRST TO GO

AFTER MY GRANDMOTHER GOT HER APARTMENT, MY MOTHER applied for Section 8. We were on a waiting list, which apparently could take years to get to us. Her government salary, especially with days off for doctor's visits, wasn't keeping up with the bills not covered by her health care.

She hadn't planned to lose the house. It was a casualty of not enough income while living in one of the most expensive cities in America.

We packed up the little yellow house, stuffed most of our belongings in the trunk and back seat of our green Nissan, and drove to our new home—an apartment on the other side of town, closer to my grandmother. It was a one-bedroom on the second floor. It had an elevator, which was good because I was still getting used to navigating stairs with my prosthetics.

"Roderick Sewell, welcome home!" my mother sang out with a smile. She knew how to make a situation seem bright.

We unpacked.

"Where are you going to sleep?" I asked.

In our house, we had our own rooms. My mother was insistent that I have my own room. She set me up in the bedroom. She wanted me to learn to be independent, and having my own room was good training.

"I'm going to sleep in the living room on the couch where the TV is," she said. "You know I like to fall asleep watching TV." I knew that, but I also knew she liked having her own room. Each morning, we would have breakfast together in the little kitchen, which had a stove and a small table in the corner. We would take the elevator, walk out the back of the building to the parking lot, hop in the Nissan, and head to school. My mom would go to work. I would go to Miss Pope's after school, and my mom would pick me up from there after work.

We had our routine. One morning, we were running late. My mother packed a little something for us to eat on the way to school. We went down the elevator and got out to the parking lot. I walked ahead of her, and when I got to the place where the car was, it was gone!

This wasn't the kind of neighborhood where people stole cars. We were friendly enough with our neighbors, and everyone had an assigned spot. Besides, who would steal an old green Nissan in a lot full of newer and nicer cars?

"Mom, the car is gone!" I said.

She didn't seem surprised. Instead, she grabbed my hand and said, "Come on!"

We were literally *running* late. And I was struggling to keep up. I was wearing my prosthetics, and I hadn't mastered walking fast, let alone running. My mom stopped, knelt down and took off my legs. She put them in her bag and told me to hop on her back. I weighed about thirty-five pounds at this point. She grabbed my school bag, her bag, adjusted me on her back, and took off running.

I was bouncing on her back, still confused. *Where were we going and why were we in such a rush to get there?*

A few blocks ahead, I saw our destination. It was a bus stop. The last person was getting on and the door was closing as my mom got there fully out of breath.

We made it! Barely.

There was a seat up front behind the bus driver. My mother plopped me down into it. Put my legs back on, while catching her breath, picked me up, and sat me on her lap. I looked around and noticed people staring at us. We must have looked like a sight to them. I had seen buses, but I had never been inside one before. It was big and crowded. Some people were wearing earphones, listening to their music on a Sony Walkman. Others were reading books or the newspaper. There were other mothers with children on the bus. Men in suits going to work.

I had questions: Where was the car? Why did we have to run for the bus? But I had learned not to ask. My mother would tell me eventually. She always told me everything eventually. But I could also tell today was not the day. So, we rode in silence to Johnson Magnet School, two stops away.

The next day, we took the same routine, minus the running. We were waiting when the bus pulled up this time. My mother was very friendly with the bus driver. Over time, the bus driver got to know us both. By the time I was eight, I could catch the bus on my own because all the drivers on our route knew me and they looked after me. I'm sure my mom arranged it all so I could get to school on my own. The seat behind the driver was always open when I got on.

The first few weeks without the car, though, my mother was there the whole ride. She walked me to my class, kissed me on my forehead, and said good-bye. Later she picked me up from Miss Pope's house, which was thankfully close to the bus stop. I got to know the drivers on the evening route, too.

I didn't like the bus at first. I definitely didn't like the people staring at me. What I hated more than the stares, though, was the waiting and the rushing. We no longer could just hop in our car and go, so we didn't go out as much as we used to. We tried to plan our trips to the store, to the laundromat, and to the movies, a routine I loved doing with my mom on the weekend. Eventually we stopped going to movies altogether.

The good thing about our neighborhood is that we had transportation options. If the bus was late, we could take the trolley, which I preferred. Riding the trolley felt like an adventure. I liked hearing the conductor over the speakers inside, the *clang, clang* of the bells, and the seating was perfect—two-seaters, enough for just me and my mom. We would take the trolley to the grocery store. In the summers, we would take it to the beach. We'd have to walk a couple of extra blocks to where the trolly picked up passengers, but I didn't mind.

The only issue was our neighborhood, which was growing less safe.

One time we were at the bus stop near Food 4 Less, a market near my school. There was also a trolley station near the street crossing, and the trolley tracks separated the Food 4 Less from the bus stop. It was around seven in the evening, and my mom and I were waiting for the bus when we heard a *pop-pop-pop!* Gunshots! Then we saw a bunch of people running. We took off running, too. Isn't that what you do when people are running?

Pop-pop-pop!

My mom slammed us to the ground. Her knee crushed into my prosthetic, and I could see the pain and fear on her face. I was confused. When it seemed as if everything was clear, she got up then helped me up. She was limping.

"If anything like that ever happens again, I need you to move as fast as possible," she said to me. I nodded my head yes. I knew I would try. But I was scared that I wouldn't be able to move fast enough to get to safety or even make it to the bus. It seemed as if we were always either waiting for the bus to come or running to catch it. And I wasn't a very good runner.

She gathered all our bags, which were scattered on the ground. We started picking up our pace walking fast toward the trolley tracks. I could hear bells in the distance letting us know it was near. If we missed that, there was no telling how long we would be waiting. We were both shaken and scared and ready to get somewhere safe. My prosthetics felt extremely heavy as I was trying to keep up. Man, did I miss our car!

A girl with long braids had run past us, but she slowed down and came back to help. This girl, who had to be no more than fourteen, grabbed our stuff and helped us onto the trolley. When the people on the trolley saw us disheveled and out of breath, they offered us a seat.

My mom sat, rubbing her leg. We got off at the next stop and walked from there to our apartment. It felt like a mile. Maybe it was just a few blocks. But that was the longest walk.

"I felt a bullet go by my head," she said.

At this young age, I fully understood that we could have been shot. And we couldn't run to get away fast enough because of me. I never wanted to feel that vulnerable again.

Chapter Six

LIKE FATHER . . .

MY FATHER STARTED COMING AROUND ONCE OR TWICE A YEAR when I was seven years old. He would come to town from wherever he was staying to see me for the day. He would take me to eat at McDonald's or someplace like that. He and my mom were cordial, but I knew my mom was putting her all into being civil. She wasn't a woman to hold her tongue for anyone, but she held it at least for the days he was in town.

My mother never bad-mouthed my father to me. And she always made sure I had a relationship with him. From as early as I can remember, as early as I was able to speak, she would put me on the phone with him. We talked just about every week. She had his pictures up around the house and she would always tell me how much I looked like him.

She also made sure I had a relationship with his family, too. He had a brother in San Diego. His mom lived in Alabama. And my mother made sure I knew them all.

We were in our apartment and had gotten used to the new schedule without a car when my father paid us a visit one Saturday. I was still in my pajamas, in front of the TV, when the buzzer to our apartment went off. We didn't have many visitors. And when my mom opened the door, there he was. I hadn't seen him in person...well, ever. Until this day.

"Great!" she said letting him in. "Just in time for breakfast!"

In walks this man, who seemed to be bigger than life. He had the same dark chocolate skin as mine, and when he saw me, he grinned. My same smile. He picked me up and gave me a big bear hug. I didn't know how to feel. I hugged him back.

He pulled up a chair and my mom made him a plate—bacon, eggs, and grits, my favorite. There wasn't much talk over the meal. I could tell there was some tension. When we finished eating, my mom cleared the dishes and said to my dad, "Are you going to tell him?"

Tell me what?

"Your dad has something to tell you," she said, chuckling. But it wasn't a *ha-ha*, funny laugh.

"Well, son..." he paused. "You, um, have sisters..." he said. And my mom let out another sarcastic laugh with a humph at the end.

But I was excited. *I have sisters?!*

"Sisters?" I repeated. I looked at him.

"Yeah...you do," he said with a nervous laugh, squirming.

"I want to meet them, now!" I blurted.

My mom and dad looked at each other, puzzled by my reaction.

At the time, I didn't understand that having sisters—three of them born all in the same year, and one of whom was born just ten months after me—meant that my father had been out there making babies with other women while technically married to my mom. But none of that mattered to me.

I had sisters! And I needed to know them. Right now!

So my dad scooped me up and put me in the front seat and we were off to meet the sisters.

I met Gina first. She lived about thirty minutes away from our apartment. Her mom is Lebanese, so she was light skinned with dark, curly hair. When she smiled, I saw my dad and my face in her cheeks. She was very friendly. She was also excited to meet me! She, too, had just learned that she had siblings.

We left Gina's house, me riding in the front seat (my dad wasn't worried about my booster seat), and Gina in the back. We went to Jonei's house, which was about fifteen minutes west of Gina's. Jonei was a little shyer than Gina, even though she was two months older. Jonei looked even more like me. She was darker and had those same cheeks. From Jonei's we headed to see Brianna. But when we got there, she wouldn't come out of the house. Actually, her aunt wouldn't let her come out and see us. She met my dad at the door while Gina, Jonei, and I waited in the car. My dad tried to convince her aunt to let her go with us to McDonald's and that it was important for he to get to know her siblings, but the answer was a firm no.

Brianna, who lived the closest to me in San Diego, was living with her aunt. Brianna's aunt was hardworking and successful— she'd recently won an award for a book she wrote. She made sure

Brianna wanted for nothing, and she was not a fan of my dad's. She deemed him too irresponsible to be around Brianna. We missed out on having Brianna in our lives—me, Gina, and Jonei—until we were in high school, when she pushed for a relationship with us. By then, I was angry about our sibling dynamic because we could have been there for each other the whole time. How could I have a sister who practically lived right down the street and not be able to talk or hang out with her?!

We have two more sisters, who are a couple of years younger than Gina. They both live in Las Vegas with their moms. And we all have an older sister, who is ten years older than me. I haven't met her yet.

To me, having more family meant more people to love. I cared more about having my sisters in my life than the adults' drama that kept us apart.

My father's brother Raymond also came into my life around this time. My mom and my uncle Ray had a rough patch in their relationship. I'm sure she blamed him for egging on my dad to hang out and party. But he was family. And since my dad wasn't around, my mom was going to make sure I knew Uncle Ray.

She let me go on a family vacation to Mexico with him and his sons, Ramond and Rashad. It was my first trip anywhere without my mom. It was a road trip in a van that looked like something Scooby-Doo, Shaggy, Daphne, and them would ride in. I was quiet most of the trip, just observing and getting to know my new family. It was about a thirty-minute drive from San Diego to Tijuana, Mexico.

I had never been out of San Diego before, and it was cool looking at the window, expecting to see tumbleweeds roll down the dirt road. It looked like something out of a wild, wild west movie. We ended up at this hole-in-the-wall restaurant that served the best tacos I have ever had to this day!

Everybody spoke Spanish, including my uncle. You can't live in San Diego without picking up some Spanish. I even understood some of what was being said, although I didn't speak Spanish myself.

My mother was good for throwing me into uncomfortable situations that she knew would be good for me in the long run. I was on a road trip practically with strangers. They didn't know me, and I didn't know them. All we knew was that we were related. I knew he was my uncle because he looked just like my father and his sons resembled me. But I was totally out of my comfort zone.

Once we got those tacos, though, I was in a great mood. The way to my heart has always been through my stomach! My uncle Ray was very engaging. He was a good tour guide, pointing out the different landmarks as we drove around Tijuana. Ramond and Rashad were two years older than me, and they were fraternal twins—Ramond looked like my uncle (and me and my dad), and Rashad must have favored his mom.

I know they must have been told about my disability before the trip because they didn't bombard me with questions as most kids would. Finally, on the way back to San Diego, Ramond broke the ice: "Does it hurt?" he asked, pointing to my legs. I had on my prosthetics.

I told him no. And that was that.

That summer, I hung out with my uncle and cousins a few more times, going to the beach and even to their house for a cookout. Uncle Ray wanted me to spend the summer with him and his two boys. Like my dad, he was a former military man. Unlike my dad, he was very devoted to being a father. And spending time with someone with that kind of discipline was needed because around this time, things were getting more tense at home.

Our housing situation was uncertain. We moved into our third apartment in six months. My mom would fall behind on the rent and before they hit us with a dispossess notice, she would find another apartment. We did this a couple of times during the summer of my seventh year. So I welcomed spending more time with Uncle Ray and my cousins. It was a stable environment.

I was living two lives though. On the one hand, there was all of this family around. And yet, my mom and I were isolated. She was becoming more and more secretive, and I could tell things were going left quickly.

Chapter Seven

TRANSITION

My mother picked me up from school and we headed to the bus stop, our normal routine. But before the bus came, she kneeled down to be at eye level with me.

"I'm going to need you to work with me today, son, okay?" she said.

I had no idea what she was talking about. But I said, "Okay."

I could tell there was a lot on her mind. She wasn't her usual playful self, hadn't been for some months now. But I learned not to ask questions.

She held on to my hand and her bag, as the words were slow to come.

What I didn't know then was that earlier in the day, my mom had packed up our latest apartment, moved our things to storage, and placed only what we needed—toothbrushes, underwear, a few changes of clothes—in that bag. This was our third apartment in six months. It had been more than three years since we left our home—the little yellow house where we shared a driveway with my grandmother. I was now a pro at taking the bus and the trolley. I was eight years old and pretty independent. I could get to and from school by myself on days when my mom had to take an early shift.

On this day, I noticed we were on a different bus, heading in a new direction, opposite the route to our apartment. This wasn't even the route to Grandma's or my aunt's.

Where are we going?

I didn't dare ask. I would find out soon enough.

We got off at a stop in front of what looked like a huge gym or old warehouse. When we went inside, there was a hallway that opened to a huge room that was filled with about thirty cots in the center.

It was quiet. People dragged along the room, many looking sad. Some were wearing layers and layers of old clothes, as if they had on all of the clothes they owned at the same time. The room smelled old and musty, and of funky body odor, too. *What was this place?*

It was strange. The people were strange. I didn't like it.

My mother squeezed my hand as we checked in with a lady at the front door. Then we set our stuff down on two cots that were next to each other. Mom seemed relieved, saying something about us getting there early enough. My mother pulled the two cots close to each other, sat down, and looked at me.

"We are going to be here for a few days," she said. Then, she handed me a brand-new Nintendo Game Boy. I spent the rest of the day getting lost in Legends of Zelda and Pokémon. I didn't even think about school or my friends. I just played and played, totally distracted by the toy that I'd been begging for all year. I played until I fell asleep on the cot.

I don't think my mom slept that night. She spent the night keeping an eye on our things and on me. The next morning, we got up before everyone else. It was around five in the morning. My mother didn't want us sharing the bathroom with anyone, and I needed extra time to wash and get ready for school. I learned that this was a shelter, a homeless shelter. This shelter was for women, children, *and* men.

When we were done washing and I was dressed, we grabbed something to eat. They had tables set up in the front of the facility with food—donuts, juice, bananas, and oranges. And there were little boxes of cereal and milk. We ate, and by 6 a.m. we were on the bus headed to my school. Mama dropped me off at school and she went to work, as if everything was normal. But I knew things were not normal—especially when after school, we went *back* to the shelter instead of our apartment.

Okay, what is happening? I had so many questions. *Why were we here? What happened to our apartment? How long are we going to be here?*

I remember my mother asking me to "work with her." What was unspoken was "and don't ask me a lot of questions and stress me out!"

So I watched and listened.

At this shelter, you had to be there before 5 p.m. to get a cot. My mom sometimes worked late, which meant we didn't get a cot that night. She'd left her government job—something I overheard her tell my grandmother one day—and was working odd jobs off the books. She also worked at a hotel doing housekeeping. She made just enough—but not too much—to qualify for the public assistance we were now on, which included food stamps and Medicaid. But Section 8, which she applied for a while ago, had not gone through. It could take years in San Diego for a housing voucher to get approved. It had taken my grandmother two years to move into that Section 8 apartment complex across town.

After our second apartment, my mom was able to secure another car—a white Honda. I was happy to be back in a car. I later learned that between the second and third apartment, she would often sleep in the car, dropping me off at my grandmother's apartment, where I could stay but she could not. Brittney and I were the only two grandkids who could spend the night at Grandma's apartment. Having the car made it easier for my mother to get around, take me where I needed to be, and go to work, and it was somewhere for her to sleep.

My mother didn't want her mother to know that we were homeless, so she told her that she had to work overnights at the hotel, and that I couldn't stay in the apartment by myself. While I was there, she was parked down the street and slept in her car. This lasted until she got us the third apartment.

Shortly after moving into the new place, the car was repossessed.

Like déjà vu, my mom told me to go to the car while she locked up the apartment. When I got to the parking lot, the car was not where we parked it the night before. When she came out and saw it was gone, I could tell she was sad. I also knew from the look on her face that the car wasn't stolen. She picked up her face and said, "Let's go. We have to catch the bus."

I was used to rolling with the punches.

When she couldn't keep up the bills for the third apartment she decided not to go to my grandma's or one of her sisters.

"My sisters had enough on their plate already," she later told me.

And I already knew she would *never* ask her mother for help like that. The choice to go to the shelter was born out of sense of independence in my mother. And perhaps some pride. It was me and her against the world. And I was on board with it. I had to be.

This first shelter was strict with the time you needed to be there. On the third night of staying there, we missed the cut-off time and the woman at the front desk wouldn't let us in. We carried all our stuff back onto the bus and had to sleep on the couch of a friend of my mother's.

We'd lost the car, but Ms. Pope was there after school picking up her grandchildren, so she took me, too. She was a buffer and a bridge and a real help during a tough time. She even let me stay there overnight some nights when my mother had to work and didn't want to bother Grandma. My grandmother, Ms. Pope, and family friends were there as much as my mother allowed, which wasn't a lot. She was trying to tough it out, to look strong and capable of taking care of me.

By the time we showed up to that first shelter, my mom had run out of options for another apartment. She couldn't gather enough money for the first and last month's deposit. She wasn't going to ask anyone for it. She couldn't ask my father, or perhaps she didn't want him to know our situation and never asked. (To this day, I don't know if he ever really knew.)

And she had run through our savings.

When we were on the verge of losing that last apartment for failure to pay, my mother had applied for us to stay at a nice shelter in downtown San Diego. There was a waitlist.

I don't remember much from this period. It was pretty much a blur.

Being the boy with no legs, I had learned to ignore things—pain, discomfort, stares—both physical and emotional. I learned to take things as they are. I learned to accept whatever I was confronted with and make the best of it.

And to her credit, my mother was good at making things feel normal and okay. She had a way about her with me that made me feel secure even in the craziest situations. I was also a little kid. And while I knew my home life was different from others my age, I had enough normalcy—school, Ms. Pope, Grandma's—that being uprooted as much as I was didn't affect me the way it probably should have.

We finally got approved for the women's and children shelter downtown. It was a complete upgrade from the warehouse. Not only were there no men, but there was also a bit of privacy and more space. They had curtains up between sets of cots, so it was like you were in your own cubicle. They also had a huge room just for the children with games and a big television. On my first night there, I made a beeline for the room with the kids. *All Dogs Go to Heaven* was playing on the television. I watched the movie while my mom got us situated. It wasn't home, but it also wasn't that other scary shelter.

I knew this was not where my mother wanted us to be. I saw the stress as we moved from one apartment to the next. I don't know exactly what happened that led us to these shelters, but I know my mom needed me to behave and be patient.

"Just work with me," she always said. And I did. In those words, she was telling me that I was her partner in this situation. I didn't feel like a helpless little kid. I was working with her, which meant we would get through it together until we had a house that was big and beautiful. My job was to not make it any harder for her. *For us.*

"I just need you to work with me. I need you to focus on school. I need your focus on your grades."

Things were easier for us in the women's and children's shelter. The people there were nice. The women looked out for each other and each other's children. It was a community. And the children all got along. I guess we were all working with our moms. My disability wasn't an issue. There were more important things for everyone to worry about than a boy without legs.

My Game Boy kept me busy. It also made me popular. All the kids wanted to play with it, and I would lend it out freely. I never worried about any of my things being stolen. We played with Pokémon cards and other games. The shelter even threw us dances and parties. I didn't dance. With my legs on, I was still awkward and stiff. But I loved watching others dance and have fun.

At Halloween, the workers threw a party. One of the workers, a guy dressed in a monkey suit, was dancing with my mom. It was nice to see her smiling and laughing again, even though the guy was dancing a little too close, if you ask me.

It was in this shelter that I discovered music. With the exception of my grandmother's blues, I didn't have many memories attached to the music and television shows many people my age loved. The 1990s and early 2000s were the golden era of rap and hip hop and television. From *The Rugrats* to *SpongeBob* to *The Simpsons* and *Family Guy*, I pretty much missed them all. I was either at Grandma's, who watched soap operas and listened to the blues, or I was at school or at the doctors' office. Although we had a television home, by the time I got back from school or being babysat, I only had time to eat dinner, do my homework, and go to bed.

I didn't grow up watching *Martin* or *Moesha* or *That's So Raven* and *iCarly*, either. While kids were taking sides between East Coast versus West Coast, Biggie versus Tupac, I couldn't name any songs from either.

At the shelter, though, they played music all the time. I remember once we were singing "Contagious" by the Isley Brothers at the tops of our lungs. I was all of eight years old, and somehow, I knew all the words, belting out, *You're contagious, touch me baby, give me what you got!* I had no idea what any of that meant, but the music brought us together, gave us something in common besides not having homes of our own.

It was fun to sing and laugh with other kids. We even went to the movie theater while staying in this shelter, which I missed doing with my mom. My mother had to work, so one of the moms took a bunch of us to see *Harry Potter*. I loved it. We shared a big tub of popcorn, with lots of butter! I became obsessed with wizards and magic after that.

In the mornings, I would slide the curtain open that separated our area from the others, and I would say, "Good morning!" to my friends before getting breakfast and heading off to school. I would try to do most of my homework while in school, but if I couldn't, this shelter had a room for kids to study and do their homework.

One of the only bad things about this shelter was that there was never enough to eat. When we had a home, I could just go to the fridge or climb up on the counter and get into the cabinet where there were always snacks or treats. I was welcome to eat when I felt hungry, and even when I wasn't. In the shelter, there was a schedule for meals, so I couldn't eat at any hour. And when the food was gone, that was it. One night in the shelter, I had a dream that I had access to endless food, that I was rich and lived in a mansion that had seventeen refrigerators. I told my mom about my dream the next day.

She laughed and then gave me a sad look. It was that day that she explained why we were in this shelter.

"I had to sell everything," she told me. "I could own nothing. I had to spend every dime to qualify for public assistance. That was the only way we could afford your prosthetics. My insurance wouldn't cover it."

It was all beginning to make sense to me now. Her sacrifice had gotten me two sets of legs already, and eventually my running legs. My mother knew I needed to have prosthetics to go to school and be productive. She explained to me that as I grew and as technology developed, I would need new legs. One leg cost more than $5,000, and I needed two every few years as I grew, and insurance would not cover them. She was determined to make the prosthetics work. She was afraid I would resent her for amputating my legs and wanted to make sure I would never have to rely on a wheelchair. I was going to walk!

She told me she applied for Section 8, and we were on the waiting list.

"This is temporary," she told me. "I will figure something out soon."

Maybe we didn't have to live in a shelter. Maybe Uncle Ray or one of my aunts would have helped if they had known. But my mom was proud—too proud to ask for help. She looked at her sisters and her mom and saw that they were dealing with their own struggles and their own responsibilities. She didn't want to be a burden to them. And maybe she didn't want anyone feeling sorry for us. So we went on this journey in secret. When we'd show up to family gatherings, we put on a happy face.

I didn't have to pretend because I *was* really happy to be with my cousins at my aunt's or Grandma's house. But no one knew we were living in a shelter, so I couldn't talk about it with anyone, even though most of my experience there was of the fun I had playing with the other children and of the moms working together to look after us all. At school, I was clean and dressed every day because we went to the laundromat every weekend. I didn't miss a day unless I had a doctor's appointment. Everything was normal, yet nothing was normal at all. It's funny what you can get used to. We were in this shelter for about a year.

One morning, mom and I left the shelter and were outside waiting for the trolley. There was a lady on the other side of the trolley tracks waiting for her ride going in the opposite direction. When she saw us, she made a beeline for me and Mom, sprinting across the tracks toward us. I could hear the trolley coming on her side, ours was still about five minutes away. My mom and I looked at her and then at each other as if to say, *What in the world is wrong with this lady? Is she crazy?!*

The woman made it to our side before the trolley ran her over. She was out of breath when she introduced herself.

"Hi. My name is Marla Knocks," she said.

Marla Knocks was a white woman who looked to be in her fifties with a short, curly bob haircut.

"I work with an organization called Adaptive Sports. It's where children like you can play competitive sports. Are you interested in playing?"

Children like me? I could tell she was referring to my disability, not my complexion.

Sports? I was active, absolutely. But I never imagined playing sports. *How?*

"Would you be interested in playing wheelchair basketball? Do you know anything about it?"

I did not. Of course, everyone knew about basketball. My friends and I all wanted to be like Kobe Bryant, and of course, Michael Jordan was the GOAT. But I had never seen a basketball game in my life, and I definitely had never imagined myself playing the sport. I didn't even know that you could hoop in a wheelchair.

"Here's my card," she said, finally catching her breath and handing my mom the card with her number. "Let's set something up. In fact, meet me at Balboa Park on Saturday. I'll be in the gym all day."

Our trolley pulled up. We thanked her and got on.

My mom looked at me and asked, "Do you want to do this?"

I shrugged. *Why not?* I was eight years old. And my entire life was about to change.

Chapter Eight

WATER WAS MY MICKEY!

WHEN YOU'RE LIVING IN A SHELTER, YOUR VIEW OF THE WORLD can become sheltered, too. I had adjusted to a "home" life that was small, insulated, and insecure. That first shelter was gray, dank, and smelly. The next shelter was better, but it was still an insulated place with rules and restrictions.

But just a mile away was a world of possibilities in the form of Balboa Park.

I had been to parks in the neighborhood, but Balboa was another world. It was twelve hundred acres and home to the San Diego Zoo. Balboa Park has seventeen museums and the most beautiful gardens I have ever seen. And the gym...Wow! The gym was a whole center that included several gyms, a track, outside fields, and several inside full courts where people could play volleyball, badminton, and basketball. It had everything.

My mom and I got up early on Saturday. We took the trolley

and the bus. And we walked for what seemed like a mile through the park. It was our first time there, and we wanted to check it out before heading over to the activity center.

"I'm glad you came!" said Ms. Marla, who jogged over to us with a smile soon after we arrived.

She and my mom talked for a while. I wasn't paying attention to them. I was in awe of what I was seeing. All throughout the gym, there were children with disabilities, just like me! Some of them were paralyzed from the waist down in wheelchairs. Some had missing limbs, like I did. All were whipping around in wheelchairs playing basketball. And these weren't the wheelchairs I saw at the Shriners Hospital. These were special. The wheels on these chairs were at an angle, slanted in toward the player. And they were fast! *This* was freedom!

"Can I play?" I asked Ms. Marla, almost out of breath with excitement.

There were a couple of empty chairs in the corner.

"Sure," Ms. Marla said. "Grab a chair."

She didn't have to tell me twice. I had never in my life been in a wheelchair—my mother was determined about that not defining my life. But in this gym, I was *excited* about using one. For the first time, I realized all you could do in a wheelchair. I took off my prosthetics, handed them to my mother, and climbed into one. It took me less than a minute to figure out what to do. My arms were incredibly strong from using them to get around half the time. I had never played basketball, but I watched the kids play for a while and picked up the game quickly.

I loved zipping around the court. The speed was amazing. As I took my first shot, I let out a "Kobe!" I missed. But it felt good.

I was playing with children who were single-below-the-knee amputees. There were kids with cerebral palsy. A couple were paraplegic. I was the only double-above-the-knee amputee. We were all playing and playing hard. There was also a lot of cheering and support and camaraderie among the players on the court.

"Nice shot," someone would say.

"You'll get it next time!" another would say.

"Foul!" Oh yeah, I was called for fouling a few times. I didn't understand the rules completely, and I may have rammed my chair into a player trying to get the ball.

Afterward, a couple of the kids told me I was really good, which was encouraging. I knew I liked to climb and ride my skateboard, but no one had ever told me I was really good at anything before this day.

After that first game, I was hooked. Ms. Marla was with Adaptive Sports, an organization that was started the year after I was born. It was partially funded by the Challenged Athlete Foundation (CAF), which has given $147 million to support athletes with physical disabilities in all fifty states and seventy countries. When Ms. Marla explained that they give grants and fund more than a hundred different sports, I wanted to try them all! I didn't even know there were that many games to play.

Seeing how excited I was on the court, my mom was all in too. They had games or practice just about every night, which was a good distraction from our actual life. In our new shelter, there wasn't the strict curfew. Several mothers worked late, and every-one respected each other. We were mostly in by nine and lights out and quiet by ten.

Despite our living situation (and maybe because of it), it was important for me to be in as many activities after school and out-side of the shelter as possible. My home life may have been chaotic and uncertain, but in sports, I found stability, structure, ground-ing, and purpose. Being with Adaptive Sports and later with CAF, I found where I belonged. I was now playing basketball after school and on the weekends. And soon I started going to CAF events all over San Diego with Ms. Marla. I loved meeting new people and being competitive.

It was through CAF that I ended up being cast as an extra in a movie, *Tears of the Sun*. The film starred Bruce Willis, who played a US Navy Seal commander who was sent to a war-torn area of Nigeria to rescue a doctor whose hospital was under siege. The doctor would go with Willis only if he and his team rescued sev-enty refugees, mostly children, some who lost limbs in the war. CAF recommended me to be one of the children.

I was the right complexion, and I was missing my legs.

My first time in Hawaii was on the set of this film. It was a six-hour flight from San Diego International to Oahu, where *Tears of the Sun* was being shot. This was my first time on an airplane, too. My mom let me have the window seat so I could see it all. The view outside my window was the most beautiful thing I had ever seen. I was amazed at the clouds and the water.

I knew for sure in that moment that there was a God. We didn't go to church or talk about religion or God, but my mother is a praying woman. It was just something that was understood. I had an encounter once in school with a teacher's aide who told me that I would get my legs back when I got to heaven. "When you get to heaven, you will be made whole," she told me. I was seven at the time. I think she thought she was comforting me, but when I told my mom what she said, my mother was so angry. I don't think that the teacher's aide was encouraging me to see my maker earlier than expected, but my mother was disturbed enough to find her and give her a piece of her mind.

For those hours in the sky, I forgot about the shelter. I forgot about ever being hungry—there was food on the plane, and the food on the set was nonstop! They had gourmet food *and* junk food—including my favorite—pizza! Now *this* was really heaven! And I never wanted to leave.

My first real hotel stay was five star! This luxury hotel had everything—two beds, snacks, a giant TV, and a shower that we didn't have to share with any other family. My mom was so happy, too. She hadn't had a vacation in like...ever. We were there for two weeks. All the hot showers, towels, and privacy in the world. Room service! Burgers and fries all day!

There was a trailer where we hung out until our scenes were shot. The director was a Black man who I later learned was Antoine Fuqua, who also directed *Training Day* and all of the *Equalizer* films with Denzel Washington. I thought that was cool. And I got to hang out with Bruce Willis in the flesh! My mom and I had to have watched *Die Hard* at least three times. It may be one of the best Christmas movies ever. He was so nice. He even took pictures with all of us.

On the set while filming I had no idea what to do. They gave us kids instructions, but I wasn't paying attention. There was too much to see. I think I messed up a couple of scenes because I couldn't keep still. The sights, the people, the *food*! It was all so exciting.

Cut! Fuqua yelled. We had to reshoot a scene where the refugees were being gathered to leave. I was looking everywhere except where I was supposed to and missed my cue. They had me on a cot with "blood"-soaked bandages wrapped around my stumps to make it look like I had survived losing my legs in an explosion. I didn't have any lines, but the scene depended on all of us following the instructions. It wasn't clicking for me.

Cut! We had to do the scene again because of me.

Maybe a part of me wanted to keep it going so I never had to leave.

My mom was in her element, too. She found a shop that sold African garb and was wearing it to match the actresses on set. I don't think either of us wanted to leave.

———

When we got back home, CAF had another surprise for me—Rudy Garcia-Tolson. He was a double, above-the-knee amputee, just like me. I didn't know that meeting him would once again change the course of my life. Unbeknownst to me, he was a champion athlete. He would become my blueprint.

CAF invited me to this major swim meet at San Diego Beach. I didn't want to go because I had a paralyzing fear of water. I wanted no part of it!

"You will not have to go near the water," my mother assured me. "But there will be other kids there like you. It will be good to see what they can do."

My mom was the ultimate hype person. She always encouraged me to do things, especially when fear was the only thing holding me back. She knew being around water was a huge discomfort for me and that this was something I needed to conquer.

"I'll be right there," she said. "It will be fun. You'll see!"

I agreed to go, but I knew that I wasn't getting anywhere near that water!

When we arrived, we walked the boardwalk. On the beach, near the water, I saw a boy surrounded by a bunch of people and cameras. He was signing autographs and taking pictures with fans.

"Who is this kid?" I thought. As we got closer, I realized that he had prosthetics on both legs. He was a double-leg amputee like me. I'd never met someone like me before.

Rudy Garcia-Tolson, from Riverside, California, was born with popliteal pterygium syndrome, a congenital condition that can affect the face, the limbs, and other parts of the body. He was born with a cleft lip and palate. He had clubbed feet that were folded over and did not function, similar to mine. His feet were webbed and so were his hands and the backs of his legs, too. He had fifteen operations by the age of five to address the cleft lip and palate and the webbed hands, feet, and legs. He later told me he was upset that they removed the webbing from his hands because that would have given him a real advantage in the water.

After the operations, he was told he would be in a wheelchair for the rest of his life. So, at five, Rudy decided he would have his legs amputated. Yes, *he* decided. If you know Rudy, you know that even at age five he was going to have his way. The amputation was through the knee, so he had kneecaps but there was no flexion of the knee.

Rudy, who was eleven going on twelve, left the crowd and approached *me*! Ms. Marla and CAF had planned for us to meet, and we hit it off immediately. We compared prosthetics—I'd upgraded from the peach-colored legs with the rubber bands to legs that were purple from the knee down, with black sockets, red knee bumpers, and yellow screws. Mine were colorful but his were way cooler. They had more features. I had never seen someone like Rudy, who was already a world-class athlete.

Rudy was a superstar. He competed in his first triathlon at the age I was—eight. He was the swimmer on a winning relay team. He had raced with comedian Robin Williams as part of Team Braveheart, which participated in CAF-sponsored triathlons. Robin Williams took the bike leg (fifty-six miles), while Rudy swam, and Ironman champion Scott Tinley did the run on Team Braveheart. By age ten, Rudy had completed the first of many individual triathlons. He would eventually win several gold medals in swimming, breaking records. And he would go on to win several triathlons after that.

On this day, he was just Rudy from Bloomington, California. He came up onto the boardwalk to meet me. I don't remember who introduced us, but I knew I wasn't going near the water. We started chatting and he led the conversation, asking me about myself and which sports I liked the best. I was still a little reserved, but we soon discovered that we had more in common than just being double-leg amputees. We liked the same music and video games. He talked about living in a trailer home and how he wanted to make enough money to buy his parents a real house. My mom and I didn't have a home at this point. I didn't tell Rudy about our situation, but I liked hearing his dreams. I also dreamed of living in a house again, one where I had a big bedroom, like the room in the hotel in Hawaii.

"There aren't a whole lot of athletes like us," he said to me. He wasn't talking about us being double amputees. He was talking about our race. Rudy is Mexican. And he told me about some of the weird stares he gets when he shows up places. I didn't have this experience...yet. But years later, when I competed in a swim meet in the South, I understood. We later bonded over that, too.

Rudy was easy to talk to. He was used to sharing his story. I mostly listened. Rudy seemed to be an extrovert. But I discovered later that, like me, he was an introvert who learned how to turn it on for the cameras and fans. Rudy preferred to stay to himself—like me! I would eventually learn by watching him how to "turn it on" for the fans and how important it was to make those connections.

We spent most of the day together, me shadowing him as he navigated the crowds. We watched a couple of the events from the boardwalk. And we became fast friends.

Rudy and I connected again several months later at a San Diego water park. *More water?!* CAF was holding a mini-triathlon and Rudy was competing. I saw him climb up without his prosthetics onto the diving platform in front of his lane. He scooted himself to the edge using his arms. He then wrapped his arms around his stumps and launched himself off the board into the pool. A perfect cannonball! I held my breath as I waited for him to come up. When he came up, he came up swimming. I watched him push off the wall using his butt instead of his legs before he kept going. He led most of the race and no one could catch him. I was like, *Whoa!*

He swam with so much joy and strength, and he came in first, of course. For me, watching Rudy swim was the beginning of something. I now saw the possibilities. Before this, the water meant sure death. But I saw Rudy swim powerfully without legs. Swim and win! *Maybe*, I started thinking, *I can swim, too.*

Through CAF, I had access to Mission Valley YMCA, near the shelter. They had free swim lessons for disabled children.

"You should try to learn how to swim," my mother encouraged me. "Why not?"

"Um, I could drown!" I said.

She shook her head and laughed. But that next Saturday we were at the Y!

At first, I just watched as the other kids swam. This Y had a big, heated indoor pool. It was nice. But I hung back and watched, promised I would get in later. I still couldn't go near the water without having a full-on panic attack.

I watched as the swim instructor, Alan, was playing swim games with the other kids. They all seemed to be having a good time. It was a mixed group—some kids had a missing leg, others had one arm, or another disability. Alan was patient and attentive to all of them. He also made it look like fun, with his big gestures and excited voice. The next time I was there, he asked me, "Are you getting in today?"

Nah! That was always my first response to that question.

"Why don't you just get in?" he suggested. "You don't have to put your whole body in. Just feel the water. Try it. If you don't like it, you can get out immediately." That day, I realized it could be more about getting used to the water and less about swimming. Understanding that removed the pressure.

I took off my legs and left them with my mom and used my arms to meet Alan at the edge of the pool. I was still petrified, but my mom gave me a nod and a smile. Alan helped to lower me onto the steps of the pool. I paused on the first step.

Okay, nothing bad happened.

I scooted from one step to the next as the water climbed up my body. I was nervous. My heart was racing. I moved like a snail, inch by inch.

Alan was right there, directly in front of me at the bottom of the steps. He didn't say a word. He just let me wig out and then figure it out. The next step put the water over my thighs, going up to my stomach. I felt out of control. I moved over to the side and grabbed the rails and held on for dear life. My mother could see me panicking and moved closer to where I was.

"We're just going to splash today," he reassured her. "I want him to get a feel for the water."

He looked at me as he moved into the pool.

"Come over to me and just splash with your hands," he said. "Just splash with your hands, and you're done for the day, Roderick."

I don't think so!

As early as I can remember, I had a fear of water. I was told that when I was a baby, a cousin who was babysitting me was giving me a bath. I slipped under and almost drowned. I don't know if that memory was lurking somewhere, but after that, whenever I would get near water as a child, I would freak out. I'm sure my fear was also attached to me not having functioning legs.

How will I save myself if I fall in? was constantly running through my head. So, when my family went to the pool or the beach, I would watch—from a distance—as everyone else got in.

"You're fine," Alan said. "You're not going to drown. I'm here. I got you!"

I was still frozen, clutching the railing. But as I looked at him, this strong, calm man who looked like he could lift every child in the water with one arm, I started to relax. He could definitely catch me if I somehow fell in. I looked at my mom and she was smiling back at me, giving me a nod that said, "you can do this."

I took a breath, rested on the steps in front of him, and splashed the water with one hand. (the other was holding on to the rail). It wasn't so bad. Nothing bad happened. But I wasn't chancing it. I quickly got out and made my way back to my mom.

The next week, Alan broke out the surfboard. *Now that's cool!* I enjoyed skateboarding, even falling and climbing back up after.

I was pretty fearless (outside of the water). But I did have my scrapes. When I was very young and hanging with my cousins, I had a really bad incident on a skateboard. We were playing at a neighbor's house around the corner from my house. They had a steep driveway, and we were riding the board from the top of the driveway to the bottom. I watched my cousins go first. When it was my turn, I didn't expect to go so fast. When I tried to stop, I put down my stump onto the concrete to stop, not thinking. I scraped the bottom so bad there was blood everywhere. I was screaming from the pain. It wasn't as bad as the time that boy busted my stitches, but it was definitely painful. My cousins and neighbor got my mom, who carried me into the house and pulled out the first aid kit. She warned me, "this is going to sting," as she poured running alcohol onto my wound.

"OUCH!" The burn was ridiculous.

She patched me up, and I was back out there skateboarding the next day...wearing my mom's Tupperware tumblers on my stumps. They were the perfect stopper.

The surfboard that Alan had reminded me of the skateboard. It was a skateboard on water. *Hmm. I could do that.* He brought the board over to the edge of the pool and told me to hop on. I did. Alan held it tightly. He was controlling it, so I didn't worry about falling off. Again, it seemed familiar. He pulled me around the water on the board, and I got more and more comfortable. I was in the water, but not actually *in* the water.

The next week, we practiced more splashing in the water while on my belly on the board. The week after that, I was putting my face in the water. The week after, I finally got *in* the water. We practiced bobbing in and out of the pool. And that was the breakthrough. I went under and popped back up.

"Oh my God, I did it!" I said, proud of myself. Up until that moment, I'd been afraid to be fully submerged. I remember water in my nose and throat and coughing. It was hard to breathe. But learning to bob reassured me that I could be underwater and survive. It wasn't as bad as I thought. Actually, it was not bad at all.

The next lessons: holding my breath underwater and blowing bubbles out my nose. Alan was a great teacher. Before long, I was going under for longer periods and popping back up, even laughing and smiling as I bobbed up and down, holding my breath on the way down, and blowing air out of my nose on the way up.

And that was it. I was no longer afraid.

Alan had toys and balls and other equipment to make the experience more fun, and for twenty to thirty minutes a session, I was in the water playing. My mother said she was so proud of me. I was proud of me, too.

This became my method for conquering my fears and trying new things. First, just try it. Second, have fun! If I could have fun, then I would continue. If it wasn't fun, I wouldn't. That's what my mom had taught me, and her advice hadn't failed me yet.

It took a minute for me to find myself in the water. Out of the water, on my skateboard or playing wheelchair basketball, I was happy-go-lucky, always smiling and laughing. At first, being in the water, I was serious and so focused on not drowning that it wasn't fun. But after a few months of working with Alan, I found the fun, and my natural personality came through. This motivated Alan to push me to do more than bobbing and playing with toys.

"Do you want to learn how to swim?" he asked.

I guess so. I'd overcome my initial fear, but now I had to keep moving beyond my comfort zone.

Alan and I started working on my technique—first out of the water. Swimming requires a lot of leg kicks. Without my legs, Alan had to teach me different techniques to get across the pool. He had to establish a solid foundation for me to learn. We started with the freestyle, where he taught me to use my hips to rotate as I learned my strokes. I would rotate with my core and hips, take a breath and glide with my arms. Alan would have me practice that out of the water first. Then he would put me in the water and had me try my strokes while supporting me, sort of like how I've seen kids learn how to ride a bike, with their parents holding them up while they pedal. Then Alan stood in front of me a few feet away and told me to swim to him.

"I'm right here," he said.

I swam a few feet, terrified. But that was it for the day.

At the next lesson, Alan moved a few feet farther. And then farther and farther each lesson, until one day, he said, "Swim to the other side. I'll be right beside you."

He walked beside me the whole way. I made it by myself. Twenty-five yards! After that, I didn't need Alan by my side. I could jump in the pool and swim. I wasn't very good, and I wasn't fast, but I could finally swim.

Learning how to swim unlocked a whole new path for my life. It would be the thing that would lead me to college and eventually to becoming a world-class athlete.

Swimming set me free!

Chapter Nine

FREEDOM!

I VISITED MY AUNT MELODY IN HOMESTEAD, FLORIDA, DURING the first few months of the pandemic in 2020. She is one of my mom's youngest sisters and the one that I became close with as an adult.

"Let's take a road trip!" she said. "There's this place in Key West with the best seafood I've ever had."

We had all been cooped up for a couple of months, and Key West was opening back up. We hopped in her SUV, just the two of us, and took the three-hour drive with joy. I'm not a big seafood lover, but there's nothing like the seafood in Key West. She took me to her spot, we ate, and afterward, we walked along the board-walk. About a mile up on the boardwalk, we were on Higgs Beach, where I noticed a plaque. It read:

African Cemetery at Higgs Beach

Near this site lie the remains of 294 African men, women and children who died in Key West in 1860. In the summer of that year the U.S. Navy rescued 1,432 Africans from three American-owned ships engaged in the illegal slave trade. Ships bound for Cuba were intercepted by the U.S. Navy, who brought the freed Africans to Key West where they were provided with clothing, shelter and medical treatment. They had spent weeks in unsanitary and inhumane conditions aboard the slave ships. The U.S. steamships *Mohawk*, *Wyandotte* and *Crusader* rescued these individuals from the *Wildfire*, where 507 were rescued; the *William*, where 513 were rescued; and the *Bogota*, where 417 survived. In all, 294 Africans succumbed at Key West to various diseases caused by conditions of their confinement. They were buried in unmarked graves on the present-day Higgs Beach where West Martello Tower now stands. By August, more than 1,000 survivors left for Liberia, West Africa, a country founded for former American slaves, where the U.S. government supported them for a time. Hundreds died on the ships before reaching Liberia. Thus, the survivors were returned to their native land, Africa, but not to their original homes on that continent.

I had no idea about this piece of history. There was this lady nearby watching us read the plaque. She was dressed in Bohemian-style clothing, with wild, natural hair. She was a real free spirit.

"You should jump in the water and take a swim and honor those who died here," she said.

It sounded like a good idea.

"But I don't have my swimsuit," I said.

"Don't let that stop you," the lady said. "Just skinny dip!"

My aunt was gassing me up, too. "Yeah, jump in butt naked!" she said.

"The water is the warmest it's been," the lady said.

I said to myself, "You know what, I'm getting in!"

There was no one on the beach this day (thank God, or I probably would not have done it). I took off my legs and left them on the boardwalk with my aunt. I climbed down to the beach and removed my shirt and shorts. I wanted to make sure they were close enough but not too close to get swept up in the waves. I moved to the edge of the water and jumped in. I swam out a bit, not too far but just far enough to float. One of my favorite parts of the water is being able to float. I love just floating in the water. Floating, I am not reminded of my disability. In the water, I am whole.

I floated on my back thinking about this being an entry point for so many people who looked like me, coming into a world of uncertainty and fear. I thought about all the people who didn't make it to these shores, whose remains were somewhere on the bottom of this Atlantic Ocean. All the hopes and dreams, stolen. All the families, torn apart.

I said a prayer for them, my eyes closed, the waves gently rocking my body. I said a prayer for myself, too. Grateful that I was free, that I am living a life no one thought I would. I turned and swam out a little farther without a care in the world.

There was a time, however, when this wouldn't be possible for someone like me.

There was a time before there was a Cullen Jones—the first Black man to win an Olympic gold medal in the swim for the United States. A time before there was a Maritza Correia (the first Black swimmer on an Olympic team). And Simone Manuel. And Lia Neal.

There was a time, not so long ago in the United States of America, when Black people couldn't go freely into the water the way I did on this day. Just thirty years earlier, it would not have been possible for me to just go into the ocean like this or even a swimming pool. And not because of my disability. There was a time when I may have died being afraid of the water because where would I have ever learned to swim and who would have taught me?

It took the civil rights movement to abolish the Jim Crow laws in the mid- to late 1960s to integrate the pools and beaches in America. Children growing up all over the United States were subjected to segregated and inferior pools and beaches... and violence. There were literally lines drawn in the sand marking where the Black people could and could not go. And if you crossed one of those imaginary lines, there was a cost. From the tragedy at Lake Lanier to the Red Summer of 1919 to the founding of Bruce's Beach, our country is full of stories that I would learn later in life. It inspires me to know it. It drives me, too, to make sure I represent and honor those who couldn't do what I do today.

I know the reason why so many Black children don't learn how to swim is rooted in a lot of that history. And it's also why Black children disproportionately drown. I encourage everyone to learn.

I cannot imagine my life without swimming today.

In the water, I am not disabled. And when I'm competing, I'm strong. I'm powerful. There are no prosthetics; it's all technique. Technique, form, and power. The water is my safe place where I can clear my mind and imagine.

In the ocean, I love floating. The waves, the weight of the seawater, it's serene. It's one of the few sports that doesn't require a teammate (unless you're doing a relay race) or much equipment besides the pool or ocean. In the pool, I love going under and finding the bottom and holding my breath. I'll grab one of the pool bricks and clap my arms over my head to get to the bottom and sit as long I can, holding my breath. It's a whole other world down there, silent and peaceful. True freedom.

Swimming has given me something, I didn't realize I would appreciate so much—a chance to connect with myself.

And a chance to be a champion!

Chapter Ten

I AM AN ATHLETE!

WHEN I WAS FIVE YEARS OLD, I TOLD MY MOM I WANTED TO BE a paleontologist. I couldn't spell the word, but after seeing *The Lost World: Jurassic Park*, I fell in love with dinosaurs. I wanted to be just like Dr. Alan Grant. I wanted to wear a cool hat and study bones in a lab.

Around age seven, I wanted to be a firefighter, like most boys my age. Everyone in my neighborhood had something bad to say about the police. I was born on the day they acquitted the police who beat Rodney King, so I understood. There was always a story or comments from my relatives about some bad encounter with the "po-po." They pulled someone over for nothing and harassed them, or they showed up in the neighborhood telling people to turn down their music. It was never anything positive.

But no one had a bad word to say about firefighters. They were heroes. As much as I could imagine how I would rescue someone from a burning building, or even save a cat that was stuck in a tree, I couldn't quite see how I could get through the training without legs.

Some of my friends said they wanted to be doctors or lawyers. I had zero desire to be either. But I could see myself as a nurse. I had been in and out of hospitals so much during my first five years of life that I had a great perspective on nurses. The doctors seemed cold and even distant. But it was the nurses who were there with a smile every time I woke up after surgery. They took care of my needs and made me feel as though everything would be okay.

When I met Rudy, though, I could see other options. Not only did he inspire me to get over my fear of water and learn to swim, but through his example I was beginning to see that anything was possible. He had fifteen surgeries before the age of five. By age six, he learned to swim, and by age sixteen he was not just competing in the Paralympic Games he had won a gold medal in the 200-meter individual medley—breaking the world record. Rudy wasn't just a good swimmer. He was an *athlete*. And his success let me know what was possible.

The summer after I learned to swim, I played a trick on my cousins. My whole life, they had only known one thing for sure: Roderick was *never* getting near any water. They had no idea I had been working with Alan and had overcome my fear *and* learned to swim well. I was staying at my grandmother's for a couple of weeks while my mother worked on finding us an apartment.

That was our routine: We would have an apartment for a couple of months, then we would be in a shelter for a few months, apartment, shelter. This went on for years.

On this day, a couple of my other cousins happened to be at Grandma's, too. It was crowded and hot in her apartment, and we were getting on her nerves. "Take your behinds outside and go play!" she yelled. We crowded out the door and heard her laughing from behind. As tough as my grandmother was, she had a soft spot for her grandkids.

My grandmother's complex was made up of two large buildings and a courtyard that connected them. My grandmother's apartment was on the ground floor of the building. From her front window, you could see an Albertson's grocery store, and there was a Blockbuster video store down the street from Albertson's. We were not allowed to go past the Blockbuster. From the building to Blockbuster, that was our range.

There was a big pool in the courtyard. The pool had a fence around it, which was surrounded by bushes. After running around for a while, my cousins decided to go swimming. We all went in, and they expected me to do what I normally would do—wait near the fence. But instead, I said, "Let's get in!" My cousins looked at me like I couldn't be serious. They thought I was joking, so I started toward the pool and scooted to the edge.

"Hey, hey...what are you doing?!" said my cousin Markus.

"I think I got it," I said. And I plunged in, clothes and all.

You should have seen the panic on their faces. They were shook! I touched the bottom of the pool and came up swimming. They could not believe it. They jumped in after me and we played for the whole afternoon. When we got back to my grandmother's apartment, I was soaking wet.

My grandmother took one look at me and said, "Boy, why are

you wet?!" She looked alarmed, mostly because of the water from my clothes dripping onto her nice floors.

"I fell in," I lied. She never would have allowed me to swim on my own. "We were playing around the pool. and I fell in."

"You what?!" Grandma said in disbelief. "Go change into some dry clothes!"

I think she threatened to beat my cousins for letting me fall in, but it was worth it to finally be able to play the games I'd missed out on all my life.

Every day I stayed there I "fell" into the pool. The first two times, Grandma believed me. After that, my mom made sure I had my swim trunks with me. She also told my grandmother the obvious, "He learned how to swim at the Y!"

I swam at every opportunity—playing with my cousins, racing at the Y, practicing techniques with Rudy and Alan. Finally, it was time for me to try my first race, a short 50 yards—down and back. By that time at age nine, my competitive spirit was in full swing. That race was a fun experience, but if I wanted to be like Rudy, the fun experience had to turn into serious work. Alan saw my potential and gave me an ultimatum: "If you want to compete in swimming, you have to give up basketball," Alan said.

Give up basketball? I was playing in a league every week and enjoying it. I loved the camaraderie, and the game was flat-out fun. But was there a future for me? I knew there was a wheelchair basketball event in the Paralympic Games, and it is very competitive. I was good, but I wasn't *that* good, even with plenty of room to learn and get better. I wasn't even close to being the best in the little adaptive sports league I was playing on.

But swimming? Could I be world class? Could I be like Rudy, who was not only winning but making a living? (He *did* buy his parents that house we talked about years earlier.)

Alan thought if I applied myself, I could.

He was very serious about training me. He saw something in me. In addition to working with disabled athletes, he also trained world-class able-bodied swimmers. And he is married to one. In 2000, Alison Terry was on her way to making history as the first Black person to make the Olympic swim team. She is a legend in San Diego.

And along with Alan, Alison Terry is one of the reasons Black and brown kids in San Diego have a place to swim. She pushed the city to keep the pools open in the inner city year-round. Alison just missed making the 50-meter freestyle in the 2000 Olympic trials. She went on to become the first Black person elected to the USA Swimming Board of Directors. I didn't know any of this when I met her. I just saw Alison as someone I could relate to. She looked like some of the people in my family, and I felt like she could understand what I might have to go through. I was glad she was around and that she would be helping to train me.

"If you do this, you have to train every day," Alan told me. "No more playing in the water. We will be doing real drills, putting in serious laps, and getting you ready to compete. I need to know you're committed."

At this point, I was still in and out of shelters and keeping it a secret. Training every day with Alan and then Alison would be a challenge. It would mean I would have to be at the pool at least five days a week. And our situation didn't lend to consistency. I told my mom about the opportunity.

"We will figure it out," my mother said to me. "We always do."

In the meantime, CAF continued to open my world, presenting me with more opportunities. On my tenth birthday, I got my first running legs. I was looking forward to it because my walking legs didn't allow me to run. At all. Thankfully, we'd only experienced the one bus stop shoot out, but I'd always wanted to play tag and race my friends during recess at school. I had been measured weeks before at the RGP Prosthetics Research Center, a facility that specialized in building limbs for people like me. They measured several times to make sure because the fit had to be perfect. These legs cost so much, there was no getting it wrong and starting over.

They took a cast of my stumps and called us when they were ready. RGP looked like a normal medical office, with a waiting room and rows of individual rooms on either side of a hallway. At the end of the hallway, the back of the facility opened up into a lab, where they kept all the tools and equipment. That was where they presented me with these thick carbon-fiber J-shaped legs where the bottom touched the ground before scooping back up into the air. I put them on, and they felt like I was walking on two pogo sticks.

In the back of the RGP prosthetics facility was a parking lot where I got to really try out these new legs. The technician asked me how they felt and whether there was any pain. There wasn't.

"Take a jog and let's see," he said.

I started running, and it was all smiles. I kept running—really bouncing and hopping—back and forth in the parking lot. It felt like I barely touched the ground before springing back up and forward. There was no knee component, so I didn't have to worry about my knee buckling and giving out. I just had to swing my legs around and make sure I landed properly, then my carbon fiber running feet would do the rest.

Walking in my running legs was weird at first, but once I started running and learning how to jump, I got used to the feeling.

"You wanna race?" I asked my mom, who was also beaming while watching me.

"Boy, you don't want this!" she said.

We lined up on one end of the parking lot.

She yelled out, "On your mark. Get set. Go!"

I took off, and so did my mom.

I was flying and bouncing as we made our way down the stretch toward the end of the parking lot. I hadn't figured out how to control these new legs yet, especially under pressure. My mom beat me! But that would be one of the last times.

I got a chance to test out my legs again the following weekend. CAF was having an event in Florida—at Disney World! I was set to compete in my first race with my new legs. The government plan my mom was on would only allow for regular prosthetics meant for walking. CAF had agreed to provide me with running legs. The tradeoff was that I would race in their events. It was a great deal for me. I got to travel and be around new people and my growing sports community. I got to compete. And I got to forget I was living in a shelter. I got to forget at least for the weekend. I had never had a foot race a day in my life (except that day against my mom). But it was an easy yes.

Disney World, here we come!

When we arrived at that hotel in Orlando, pictures of Mickey and Minnie and Goofy were all over the lobby. We checked in, and as the night went on, I started getting nauseous. I was also running a fever and had a really bad headache. By bedtime, I was sick. The doctors on site said I was suffering from dehydration. I must have forgotten to drink water all day while traveling. My mom was freaking out, so she sent someone to the drugstore to get me some Pepto Bismol, children's aspirin, and a ton of water. The next day, I was still weak. But I'd come all the way across the entire country for this. I was going to race.

On the track, I had no idea what I was doing. I had not trained at all. They told me to go to the starting line, where there were four other kids. I was the only double-leg amputee.

"When you hear the gun, go," said the race organizer.

I had no technique and zero form. And I hadn't really figured out how to use the legs yet. When the gun went off, I started hopping along, using the curved bottoms of the legs to spring me forward. I alternated between hopping and running. I must have looked like a mess. My saving grace was that it seemed as if the other runners, who were all elite athletes, had issues with their prosthetics. Before the first turn, one kid's foot broke off. Another kid's foot came loose. And another, a single-leg amputee, had his entire leg come off. By the end of the race, the track was littered with prosthetic limbs—except for mine.

For the first time in my life, I felt as if I had an advantage. I had the privilege of being a CAF athlete, and the fancy running blades made a difference. Without any experience or training, I won my first race! I was proud showing off my first-place medal to my cousins and friends and telling them how I beat these elite athletes. (I didn't bother mentioning how I actually won.)

My mom was in the stands screaming her head off. I could hear her over all the other fans and noise. I got a trophy and a medal that would end up in a storage unit because we didn't have space at the shelter. But I was so happy. I couldn't wait to run more and master these running blades. Running made me feel like I was flying! I loved it.

I really loved playing basketball. I loved being a part of a team. Should I give up basketball and now running? And focus on swimming? I didn't want to. But I knew I needed to. Because swimming could give me a future, a career.

I was leaning toward training with Alan. But at that time, my mother and I were making it to the gym when we could. It was a challenge to show up every day when we didn't always know where we'd be coming from or headed to at the end of practice. I looked at Alan and Alison cheering in the stands. I wanted to train with them, but I couldn't commit, so I could not promise. I could tell his interest in training me was waning. He looked at me as flaky. But I couldn't tell him why. But my mother finally said, "I think we need to talk to them."

Back in San Diego, Alison and Alan invited us to dinner at a pizzeria after practice one day. It was there that my mom finally explained our situation. We had been going to swim lessons at the Mission YMCA off and on for almost two years. I was ten years old, and now that Alan was pressing me to take swimming seriously, he needed to know that we were unhoused and our transportation to the pool every night would be a challenge.

They were surprised, shocked actually.

"What can we do?" Alan asked, looking at Alison with an expression that said, "We *can* do something!"

"You guys have done enough," my mom said. "You gave Roderick a tool a lot of people don't have. He can swim. He is not afraid. And he will always have that. Thank you!"

Mom was right. They *had* done enough. We hadn't asked for anything in my years of working with CAF. I was happy to be able to do all the things I had been exposed to. And on that night, I was just happy to be out eating pizza. But Alan Voisard and Alison Terry were not the type to leave the matter there. They sort of adopted me and my mom after learning about our situation. They made sure I was at practice five days a week, even if it meant they had to pick me up.

We ended up spending the holidays with them at their house in the rich part of San Diego. My mom and I stayed with Alison and Alan, and we went with them to Alison's dad's house for the Christmas festivities. He had a huge house that was so big it had multiple wings. I could get lost there. We met Alison's dad, his wife, and Alison's siblings. Alison's mom was there with her partner. And Alan's mom. The house was so big that everybody had their own room.

Christmas morning was amazing. The tree had to be about fifteen. It looked like something you would see at the mall. I had never seen a tree like that in somebody's house. It was so different from what I was used to. Mom told me when I was four years old that *she* was Santa Claus, the Tooth Fairy, and the Easter Bunny all in one! The first Christmas I remember, mom broke out a small, plastic tree that we decorated together the night before. We had black angels and red and green-colored ornaments, no lights and a silver star on top. My mom made sure there were two gifts under the tree—one for me and one for her. She cooked breakfast and would play old Christmas songs from people like Lou Rawls and the Temptations. She and I would sing to the top of our lungs! One Christmas, I got five gifts instead of the usual singular present. A few family members contributed to the bounty. But as I got older, and especially when we were in the shelter, it was just me and her exchanging a gift apiece.

At Alison and Alan's, there were presents for days. There was something for everybody under that tree. I got a PlayStation 2! While I tried to get the PS2 plugged in and booted up, Alison and Alan handed my mom a little box wrapped in white wrapping paper with a little bow on top. She looked at it hesitantly. I don't believe my mother had a good Christmas growing up, and I don't remember anyone ever giving her a gift wrapped so nicely.

But what was inside was beyond anything she or I could have expected.

It was a key. A BMW key! My mother started crying.

Alan and Alison had an old BMW that they didn't use any-more. Instead of selling it, they gifted it to my mom. For the first time in a long time, when we left their home, we drove back to our own apartment. My mom had found a place in El Cajon a few months prior. We were there for less than a year, but during that time, I was able to get to swim practice consistently. I gave up all other sports and committed to becoming a swim champion.

After we opened the presents, we played a hardcore game of Uno. Competitive athletes play everything hard. Alison was brutal with that reverse card! She hates to lose almost as much as I do. After fun and games, we made our way to the dining room for the most amazing meal I had ever had. They had everything—ham, turkey, greens, potato salad, macaroni and cheese, cornbread, and biscuits. And every dessert you can imagine from chocolate cake to apple pie. I ate until I almost burst (I may have eaten five of those biscuits by myself). What a Christmas!

———

I was heading to middle school in the fall, and if I was going to be a swim champ, I needed to go to a school that would prepare me for a good high school and eventually college. My local middle school fell short in every way.

My mom once again stepped up. She applied for and got me a scholarship to Nativity Prep Academy, a much better school. The school was closer to the Mission Y, within walking distance, making it easy for me to train every day right after school. Not only was Nativity Prep conveniently located, but it was also one of the best middle schools in San Diego. It touted on its website, "Nativity Prep students are 5x more likely to graduate from college than other historically underserved students." That meant I would be ready for college, too.

Alan went from my swim instructor—playful and fun—to my coach—strict and demanding. Gone was the smiling, easygoing Alan, replaced by a no-nonsense drill sergeant who demanded excellence and discipline. I was no longer a kid scared of the water. I was now a competitor. It was a different thing. His personality didn't change as much as his methods. He was still a nice guy but one who smiled a lot less. He was focused. And I had to be focused too—and serious. He set the tone for me. I made a commitment, and he expected me to honor it. There would be no more playing in the water. And no excuses.

My mom now had a car, so she was expected to pick me up from the pool after practice and make sure I was at any event I had to compete in on time. Sometimes she would get there early to wait and stay late and watch me wrap up. For two hours a day, I was swimming. We worked mostly on technique. Most of the strokes—freestyle and breaststroke—rely on a strong kick. I had to make up for my lack of kick with perfect technique and arm and shoulder strength.

In February, I swam in my first meet. It was the Black History Invitational Swim Meet, a Black History Month event held annually in Washington, DC. I traveled with Alison and Alan, nervous and definitely unprepared. But like everything I conquered in the water with Alan, I knew this would be an experience that would get me closer to my goals.

I had trained, but I was still growing as a swimmer and I wasn't very fast. Alan wanted me to experience competition—with swimmers who weren't disabled. "I don't expect you to win," Alan told me. "I expect you to get better."

We did a mini-tour around DC. I saw the Lincoln Memorial and the Washington Monument in the morning before the race. This three-day invitational hosted kids from ages five to eighteen, competing in everything from relay to all of the strokes. Children came from Atlanta, Detroit, New York, and, like me, from California.

I hadn't been anywhere like this. It was crowded, and there were Black people everywhere. "Chocolate City" was an understatement.

In CAF, most of the athletes were white. Most of the events were put on by and sponsored by and supported orgs led by white people. I was growing up and realizing some things, especially the kinds of looks I would get at events. When everyone is disabled but you're singled out, you begin to know that your disability isn't the problem. But I always ignored the stares and the whispers at practices and meets. This event in DC was the first I attended where the majority of people around me were Black. They didn't say so, but I think Alan and Alison wanted me to see this. It was refreshing to see so many children who looked like me. I was one of the few children there with a disability. In fact, in my event, the 100-meter freestyle for kids thirteen and under, I was the only amputee.

I walked over to my lane on my stumps, and I waited for the whistle to blow. When I heard the familiar beeping noise, I plunged in and started my stroke, concentrating on rotating my hips and grabbing a breath. I was methodical and very slow. I got to the end of the pool for the first length, but I hadn't yet mastered the flip. So, I just pushed off with my stump and headed back to the other end. It seemed like a mile away. I got there, turned and I saw swimmers heading back my way. I had been lapped by at least two swimmers. By the final length, I saw that every other swimmer had hit the wall and was done. I had to finish. As I pushed off a final time, I could hear the crowd cheering me on. Every time I emerged to take a breath, I heard, "GO!" and "You got this!"

By the time I got to the wall, people were clapping and yelling words of encouragement. I came in dead last. Of course, I was still embarrassed by how slow I was. But it felt good to have a room full of Black swimmers, Black coaches, and Black parents from all over the United States cheering for little Black me.

After we returned to San Diego, I was fired up to take my training to the next level. Next year, I wasn't coming in last! Alan was on board, too. He wanted me to train with a team of able-bodied swimmers so I would get used to the rigor. He said they would make me better.

"Teamwork makes the dream work," he said. It was corny but true!

Fighting for a team instead of just fighting for me and my individual pursuit would give me more depth and drive. I was looking forward to it.

Chapter Eleven

"WE'RE MOVING TO ALABAMA?!"

IN DECEMBER 2004, MY MOM HIT ME WITH ANOTHER CURVEBALL.

"We're moving to Alabama!"

What?!

Despite all the help we received from Alan and Alison, we were still living between apartments and shelters. I was beginning to think that there was something more going on than just being low on funds all the time. I couldn't understand it. I know my mom applied for Section 8. I know my grandma got her voucher years ago. Up until this point, I simply did what she needed me to do. I worked with her. But this latest move was wearing on me.

We spent the longest stretch, almost the full previous year, in one particular shelter—St. Vincent De Paul in San Diego. I had a routine there. I'd go to school, which I enjoyed a lot. After school, I would train for at least two hours with Alan. My mom and I would grab something to eat after that—usually fast food. And then it was back to St. Vincent DePaul, which was starting to feel like home. I would be so exhausted when we got there, I usually crashed after taking a shower each night.

I liked my routine. And I liked what was happening with my body. I was getting faster and stronger—stronger than I could imagine. Alan worked with me not only on my technique and my breathing but also my strength. And I loved the results, more wins, stiffer competition.

How could I train and compete in Alabama?

We had just come back from Washington, DC, where I competed and did pretty well in my first-ever swim meet. Alan had created a plan for me that included at least one meet a month. There was even an appearance at a CAF event with Rudy where I would be asked to talk about my experience as an athlete. Things were happening.

And things were ending.

My mom broke the news to Alan and Alison.

"We're moving to where Roderick has family and where I can finally get us on our feet," she told them.

They didn't say anything for a long pause, probably a mix of sad and angry. Finally, Alan said, "We're going to miss you!"

Alison just shook her head.

I could tell they were both not feeling my mom in this moment. A couple of months before this announcement, she sold the car they gave her. She said she needed the money.

"We will figure out how you will keep training," Alison said. "I have some connections in Alabama."

But I could tell, things were about to change...and not for the better.

My mother told me that we were moving to Alabama because things would be easier. The cost of living was way less than in San Diego apparently. And we had family there, too. That's where my other grandmother, my dad's mom, lived. My uncle Ray also moved back home with the twins. My mom had a job lined up and said that we would be staying with my grandmother until we found a place of our own.

I was dreading the move. I was just getting in my groove as a swimmer. I was the most fit I had ever been, and I had friends I was close to. We were scheduled to leave on a Friday after school. My mom asked me to come straight "home" to St. Vincent DePaul because she had some last-minute things to take care of before our bus for Alabama left at six that evening.

School let out at three, and I thought it would be okay to hang out with my friends and say good-bye. I didn't know if I would see them again. My cousin Brittney and my sisters Gina and Jonei met at my friend Robert's house. His mom ordered pizza, and we played video games and had a good time. After a few hours, we were interrupted by Robert's mom, who came into the family room and told me my mom was on the phone.

I didn't have a cell phone. And I hadn't told her I would be hanging out after school because I didn't want her to tell me no. She had no idea where I was and I knew she would be pissed, but when I took the phone from Robert's mom, she was yelling at me like she never had before. She apparently was worried out of her mind and had called everyone she knew looking for me. Robert's mom dropped me off at the bus stop. When I got there, my mom was visibly frantic and upset.

"I needed you to be here!" she said. She was shaking with anger.

"I thought it was okay to spend some time with my friends since I wouldn't see them for a while," I said.

"I asked you to come straight home! I said, come straight home!"

I didn't know what to say.

"We lost everything," she said.

I had no idea what she was talking about.

She explained that the storage unit where all of our stuff was closed at five. It was now five-forty. We would not be able to get our things. She didn't have enough money to store them for an extra day. And even if she did, we didn't have the time. Our bus was leaving in less than thirty minutes, and the storage place would be closed until the next day. She'd scraped together all the money she could for the move to Alabama. She'd even sold the BMW Alan and Alison had given her so we would have enough to live on for a while.

We were now traveling very light. Gone forever were the trophies and medals I had won competing for CAF. Gone were family mementos and photos, many of my baby pictures, my mom's journals she had been keeping where she would write out her dreams and fears, and other personal items she couldn't keep with us in the shelter. Our life in boxes. Gone.

Those boxes in storage had always represented hope that one day we would be stable with a home of our own again. Those boxes in storage were going to be the seeds to us returning to a normal life in a new location. Instead, we were starting this next journey the way we had gotten through most of my childhood—with nothing. It devastated my mom, who had been holding it together as we navigated apartment after shelter after apartment all these years. Not coming straight home that day is one of the biggest regrets I have.

At 6 p.m., we got on the bus. We found two seats in the middle on the bus driver's side and traveled almost two thousand miles across the country—two whole days. We slept on the bus, and we ate along the way at rest stops. It was the longest trip I have ever taken by bus—made longer by the silence. My mom was unusually quiet. She certainly had a lot on her mind. She hadn't discussed much of the plan beyond the bus ride.

We arrived in Alabama in the middle of the afternoon, and the first thing I noticed was the weather. January in San Diego would be in the 60s. I never needed a coat. We got off that bus and the cold hit me in the chest. My mom took a jacket out of our bag and we both layered on the clothes. When I thought about the South, I didn't picture cold.

The other thing I noticed was the pace. Everything was slower in Alabama. Even the way people talked. It felt like we'd landed on another planet in another time. There wasn't that hustle-bustle, and the streets were empty in comparison to San Diego. Everything was just so different.

We stayed at a hotel for a couple of nights. Turns out, mom's plan was to arrive in Alabama and figure it out. She connected with my aunt Brenda, Uncle Ray's ex-wife. They were really good friends. I guess they bonded over their marriages to two brothers.

My aunt Brenda invited us to stay with her and my twin cousins I hadn't seen in years. They looked like grown men, fourteen and huge. My mom and I shared a room. There were always activities in the home and voices booming throughout. I loved staying there at first. I got to learn a bunch of video games and had someone to hang out with. Ramond and Rashad were very competitive, both of them hated to lose—at anything. At first, I found it amusing when a fight would break out over an NBA 2K game or a card game where one of them accused the other of cheating. But the arguments would turn to tussling and then to fisticuffs. One time they put a hole in the wall.

"How are we going to fix this?" said Rahman, looking at me and Rashad.

We? I had nothing to do with it!

Rahman and Rashad were always getting into something, fighting all the time. It was fun to watch, at first. But I wasn't used to it.

On Sundays we would all go to Grandma Rozell's for dinner. My uncle Ray stayed there with her to take care of her. It was nice to be with family. And the food was amazing. After one Sunday, my grandmother said to my mom, "Why don't you stay with us here? We have plenty of room."

It was a bit crowded there. Aunt Brenda was so gracious and kind, but there was also a lot to handle with three teenage boys, two of whom were playing on their high school football team and were rough as heck. They needed their space, and at thirteen, so did I.

Grandma Rozell, who I called just "Grandma," was very different from my mom's mom. Grandma Rozell was reserved and proper. She was a churchgoing woman. Before meeting her, I would speak to her on the phone a lot. And, of course, my mom would show me photos of her. In every photo, she had a regal expression, hands folded in her lap, very conservative. She was just like her photos in real life. She did give me a big hug when she saw me, though. She seemed happy to see us.

My grandma Rozell had lived in this same house most of her adult life. She'd raised my dad and uncle in this house. Living there, I realized that my dad grew up in a nice home with parents who cared, and that he was sort of the black sheep of the family.

Grandma Rozell's house was immaculate. Clean. Everything was in its proper place. She had silverware and dishes that matched. There was a curio in the dining area where she stored her china. Curtains hung from every window. There was even a sitting room where no one was allowed to sit. It had a bone-white carpet and plastic on the furniture. She called it the show room. I made the mistake of going there with my prosthetics on, not thinking about the dirt on the bottom of them. She didn't yell at me, but the look she gave told me I had better not ever go in that room again.

Uncle Ray cleared out an old office, and we slept on a blowup mattress for a couple of weeks before getting a bed.

After the newness wore off, things started to settle into old ways. My grandma was very critical of my mom's lifestyle. They would get into arguments, and my grandmother seemed to always defend my dad and blame my mother. My mother would state the obvious—that my dad wasn't contributing to her life or mine—and my grandmother would find a way to put our unsteady living condition solely on my mom. She would nitpick and throw little comments toward my mom, which would illicit a "Don't you go to church? Is this Christian-like?" from my mom, who never bit her tongue when challenged.

I wasn't happy living there. I missed San Diego. I missed my friends. I missed my school. And mostly I missed training.

It didn't take long for one of those arguments, which Uncle Ray would sometimes join in, to blow up into a "I'd rather stay in a shelter than stay here!"

And the next day, we were packing up and leaving again...for a shelter.

Chapter Twelve

GREENS, MACARONI AND CHEESE, CHICKEN, BISCUITS . . . YOU NAME IT!

I MUST HAVE PUT ON FIFTEEN POUNDS IN THE FIRST MONTH we moved to Alabama. I went from dreaming about seventeen refrigerators and feeling hungry all the time to eating anything I wanted, as much as I wanted.

Both Grandma Rozell and Aunt Brenda could throw down in the kitchen. And as much as I didn't like being in Alabama, the food was making it bearable. Every day seemed like Thanksgiving—only better. There were mashed potatoes and fried chicken, greens and biscuits, macaroni and cheese, pork chops. And all the sweet tea I could drink. I never had tea like this in San Diego. Everything was fried and everything was delicious. I went from eating on a schedule in the shelter to eating whenever I wanted when I was with family. I couldn't get enough when I was there.

By summertime, I realized that the South's heat was different.

I was used to California's hot weather, but this Alabama heat was oppressive—moist, humid, and harsh. In just a month, we went from the coldest I had been to the hottest.

I focused on the food. I was not just out of shape; I was a little butterball, as my auntie liked to say.

I had stopped training altogether. The nearest YMCA was several miles away from my grandmother's house. It wasn't like San Diego where you could hop on a bus or trolley and go just about anywhere in the city. Alabama was different. Everything was far, public transportation wasn't convenient, and there weren't a lot of training facilities.

Alan and Alison checked in on me every few weeks. They were concerned that I wasn't able to work out and keep up with my training. But they were even more concerned about my struggles in school.

I started at Davis Middle School in Fairfield in January, right in the middle of sixth grade. This school not only lacked facilities for me to train but also had zero provisions for people with disabilities. There were no handicap ramps and no handicapped bathrooms. I could get around without the ramps, but I definitely needed access to a bathroom. My mom kicked up a fuss in the front office. She threatened to go to the press. Within a few weeks, they had installed some makeshift bars in the bathroom, handrails leading to the second floor, and a ramp leading into the school, thanks to Mom.

But the school itself, the curriculum, was also a problem. They seemed to be at least a couple of years behind San Diego. Of course, I should have just breezed through. But instead I was extremely bored, and the thick southern accents of my teachers drawled on. I would sit in class and daydream, and pretty quickly my grades showed it.

"You will not be able to go to college if you let your grades slip," Alan told me during one of his check-ins. My mother shared with him my struggles.

College? I hadn't ever really considered going to college. I had thought that one day, perhaps, I would be a nurse because I loved to help people. And I guess, I knew I would need to go to school for that. But college seemed so far away.

"Bad grades now will follow you later," Alan warned me.

I shared with him that much of my struggle wasn't because the school was hard—just the opposite. I was falling behind because I couldn't understand my teachers and because I was bored. Much of what they were teaching I had already learned.

"Then challenge yourself," he said. "Make it hard. Find something that interests you. And dive into that. And if it's so easy, then I expect you to prove it by getting good grades."

Alan knew exactly how to get me motivated. *Challenge accepted.*

I figured if I was going to live in Alabama, I should know everything about Alabama.

One of the first weeks in class, we watched a documentary called *Eyes on the Prize.* I had never really known about the history of the civil rights movement and how Birmingham—where we were now living—was one of its epicenters.

I learned about the 1955 Montgomery Alabama bus boycott that was started by the NAACP after Rosa Parks was arrested for refusing to give up her seat on a bus. I later learned that she wasn't the first person to refuse to get up. There was Claudette Colvin, who was also was arrested for not giving up her seat to a white person. She did this nine months before Rosa Parks. But she was only fifteen years old and pregnant and unmarried.

I learned about the bombing of the 16th Street Baptist Church in 1963 where four young girls were killed by racist terrorists in Birmingham. There were the Freedom Rides of the 1960s and Bloody Sunday on March 7, 1965, when hundreds of Black demonstrators attempting to march to the state capital in protest of police brutality were brutally beaten and teargassed on the Edmund Pettus Bridge by police. Hosea Williams and John Lewis, who would go on to become a US congressman, led the way. There was the Dexter Avenue Baptist Church in Alabama, where Martin Luther King Jr. got his start as a preacher in Montgomery.

All that history was right there, and I knew very little of it until the year we moved. Of course, I understood racial tensions. I was born on the day of the LA Riots and was used to being stared at at competitions in San Diego for being the only Black kid. But I'd never connected the dots. I didn't understand how racism was deep, systemic, and present *everywhere* in the United States.

Where we stayed in Fairfield, just outside Birmingham, everyone was Black. I wasn't used to that. San Diego had a little bit of everybody. My classes there had kids of every race. But Alabama was and still is very much segregated. It was still very Black or white depending on the neighborhood you were in.

I finished the sixth grade at Davis Middle School with decent grades. Then I started Forest Hills Middle School in Bessemer for the seventh grade. By this time, we had moved out of my grandma's house (my mom wasn't playing) and were in our first Alabama shelter.

My mom thought moving to Alabama would be easier, that she would have so much support. And she did. It was easier in some ways. But it was also harder than she expected.

The shelter system in Alabama was similar to the one in San Diego. It was actually better because there were fewer people. The first shelter we stayed in housed only three families. We shared a bathroom with the other two, so we scheduled with each other when we wanted to use it. They were very nice, and we still stay in touch with one of the families we met there.

At this point, my mom was an expert in navigating "the system." She went to family services and applied for Section 8 housing. She then took me to Birmingham's public transportation office and applied for Access-A-Ride. You had to show you have a disability. I was standing right there, so of course, they approved us.

Access-A-Ride was a lifesaver. I used it to get to school, and I was able to start training again, which I desperately needed for the structure and the fitness.

While we were back in the shelters, it was a little different this time. The shelters were well kept, and the staff were required to rotate families every month. We were never allowed to stay in one shelter longer than a month. In the first one, there were three families. The next one had two. We were in the Bible Belt, and churches would work with the shelters to provide food and clothing and volunteers.

Every Sunday, someone would open their home to us for Sunday dinner. The organizers of the shelters had an arrangement with different churches where families would invite different shelter families over for Sunday dinner. My mom and I really enjoyed meeting different people. And I, of course, enjoyed the food. I don't think I had a bad meal the whole time in Alabama. It was as if everyone knew how to cook.

Our third shelter rotation had us with four families. We had beds, books for kids. It was nice. They had a TV that we all shared. In one of the last shelters we stayed in, one of the workers said he was Ruben Studdard's uncle. I love Ruben Studdard! I busted out singing, "I Need an Angel." He joined me and we had a ball!

The six months in Alabama's shelter system was a breeze. It flew by. Then we got the call. An apartment was ready and available for us! The call came while we were on our way to the bus stop. Sometimes we didn't want to wait for Access-A-Ride to show up, and the city bus was more convenient for getting around and running errands.

I was walking ahead, and I noticed my mom wasn't with me. I looked and she was frozen in the spot where she got the call, bawling. She was crying her eyes out, so I walked back to her and held her in my arms. It was as if all of the pain she was holding in, all of the disappointment and anger was just flooding out of her in that moment. We got an apartment!

"We're going to be alright," she said through sobs.

Her experience in Alabama wasn't the best. From living with her ex-sister-in-law to living with her ex-husband's mother to being homeless again. But getting that call, she knew with certainty: "We're going to be okay!"

We moved into a brick building duplex. There were clusters of duplexes in this neighborhood in Fairfield. Ours was toward the back, near the parking lot, and it was away from the others, which I liked. It was right next to a church. It was an adaptive apartment, so it had a ramp instead of steps leading to the front door and rails inside along most of the walls, including in the shower. I didn't use the rails much; I had gotten used to not having them. But I was glad the building managers made sure we had what we needed.

Everything was falling into place. I was fourteen and needed a new set of prosthetics. Hanger Clinic in Birmingham was one of the best in the area. That's where I got fitted for my new legs. My prosthetist, Reggie, was Black! It was the first time I had a prosthetics technician who was Black. And he was meticulous, making sure every detail and measurement was exact.

When I got my new legs, I had to relearn how to walk. The technology had improved since my first set of legs. I went from having mechanical knees, which I had spent years getting good at, to hydraulic knees. They were far more advanced and also tricky at first. The mechanical knee operated when I lifted my heel a certain way. I had the rhythm down. The hydraulics were automatic and jarring at first, and not as fun as my first few times using running legs. Jason let me practice, but those few minutes in the office weren't enough. "Like with everything, practice makes perfect," I remember him saying.

The next day, I was on my way to school. The Access-A-Ride

van was waiting for me. I left the house and started walking toward the van when I fell. My mother was in the doorway of our place, watching. I picked myself up and walked a few steps and fell again. *Whew.* The van driver looked concerned. I was several feet from the door of the van, and I know the driver wanted to get out and help me. But I put up a hand, got myself up and started again. I fell again.

The third time, I got it. I stood, and let the hydraulics do their thing. They made the adjustment for me. I was used to doing all of the work. Now I didn't have to. I took a step and then another and another. I was walking! I made it onto the van and to school and didn't fall again that entire day.

The neighbors were also watching that morning. They saw my mother allow me to fall, and they called child protective services because they thought she was being cruel by not helping me. They didn't understand how important it was for me to learn how to walk in these new legs and that the only way to learn was to do it. My mother and I had been through this routine several times—at CAF events, family gatherings, at home trying to get my balance right. She was there. She was watching. She knew what I needed. She also knew that *not* helping me walk was the only way for me to master walking. From the outside, it looked like abuse and negligence instead of practiced love and care.

But my mother was making sure I could stand on my own two feet!

Chapter Thirteen

BREAKING THROUGH AND A BREAKING POINT

"Let's go!" my mom said on Saturday. She was tired of me sitting around the house being lethargic and eating. She had called Access-A-Ride, and they dropped us off at Lakeshore. Lakeshore, a Paralympic and Olympic training facility in Birmingham, was recommended to us by some folks we'd met through CAF. My mom made arrangements when she first knew we were moving to have us connected to a training facility, but it had taken almost a year for her to get stable enough for us to make the move. It was long overdue.

Before leaving California, I was starting to fill out with muscles. Now, I was just a ball of fat. And it was affecting my behavior. My mom knew getting me back into sports would help.

Lakeshore was smaller than Balboa Park, but it had everything. It had a couple of basketball courts for the wheelchair basketball team. It had a track for runners and cyclists and a swimming pool.

It was where para-athletes in the area trained for the Olympics and triathlons.

My first day in the pool was rough. I hadn't swum in eight months, and the extra weight wasn't helping. Swimmers are lean and long. I was round. I told Alan and Alison that I would swim in the Black History Month meet in DC again in February, but I couldn't show up out of shape and out of practice. And I definitely didn't want to place last. Not again.

Before I left San Diego, Alan was talking to me about joining a swim team there. Lakeshore in Birmingham had a swim team made of all para-athletes. There were kids with spina bifida and cerebral palsy. I was the only double-leg amputee. Alan was right. It was better swimming with a team. I was used to doing everything solo. It was nice to have others to rely on, to help me refine my technique, and just to talk with.

I had not made many friends in Alabama. I saw Rudy only once a year at the CAF fundraiser. And I talked to my cousins back home, but not much. And since we moved out of my dad's mom's house, we didn't see his family that much. It was just me and my mom.

Every weekend, and a couple of days during the week, I was at Lakeshore. I was building a little community there. I got back into wheelchair basketball. On the swim team was Daniel, who competed with Rudy in the Paralympic games. He was cool. Week by week, I was finding my joy again.

For my mother, this was important. She could tell I wasn't myself for most of our time in Alabama. My only happiness seemed to be in food. But sports was where I could find happiness.

I trained every week with the Lakeshore swim team leading up to my second appearance in the Black History Month Meet in DC. I was looking forward to seeing Alan and Alison. It had been almost a year. When we arrived in DC, they met me and my mom at the airport. Alan only said, "Let's get you back active again!" We had a great time catching up.

The next day was my race—the 100 meter. I was in the thirteen-and-up group. And once again, I was the only disabled swimmer. Before the race, Alan gave me a pep talk.

"Don't forget to pace yourself," he said. "Remember, the first length you come off the blocks fast, come off that wall, and then coast on the second length. On the third length, you want to pick up the pace. And that final length, you know what to do. Bring it home! You got this!"

I nodded. I just knew I didn't want to come in last again.

On your mark…get set…

GO!

I hit the water, using my upper body strength to propel me through. I made it to the wall. I was in last place but not far behind the pack. I kept pace with them. Heading into the third length, I noticed there was a swimmer behind me! I wasn't in last anymore! I knew I had to pick it up because if he got to the wall before me, he'd be able to kick off and get ahead of me. I couldn't let that happen. I pushed off and when I came up, he was still behind me.

The crowd was on their feet again as I headed to the finish. This time, it wasn't just to encourage the boy with no legs. This time, they were cheering on a real race. They were cheering the show of competition they'd come to see. The boy behind me was gaining on me, but I was close to the end. Could I stay ahead of him? Would I finish last again? The cheers were now roars. People were on their feet.

My adrenaline was through the roof. I pulled and stretched with all my might, and I reached the wall. I beat him. I didn't come in last!

I was so thrilled.

My dad was one of the people in the stands. He and his wife came to see me. They lived in Virginia and drove up just for this. He was newly married to a woman he met while he was in the military. My mom liked her. She kept my father in line and made sure he did the things he needed to do. He was really trying, thanks to Mama Deborah (my mother liked her enough to allow me to call her that).

Between not coming in last, the crowd's encouragement, and having my dad present, I was on cloud nine. This was my first time he got to see me compete. And I beat someone who didn't have my challenges. Rudy did it all the time. In fact, in his speeches, he talks about beating this kid when he was eight years old. "I'm pretty sure that kid went to therapy after being beaten by a boy with no legs," he would joke.

This was a first for me. I felt like I could compete against anyone—disabled or not. And I wanted to, as much as I could. I loved my community at the Lakeshore and the CAF's competition circuit. While we were leaving, I was thinking about everything I could do in sports when my mom and I overheard the boy I beat trying to make an excuse to his about why he lost to me. For a second, I doubted myself, till I heard his mother's response. She wasn't having it.

"No. You weren't prepared, son," she said. "And you underestimated him."

It wouldn't be the last time someone underestimated me and got surprised. It certainly wasn't the first either.

A few weeks after seeing me compete, I got a call from my dad. He had been apparently keeping up with my accomplishments through the press and on Facebook. CAF posted a lot of my competitions and how well I was doing, they posted the upcoming races.

"I see you have a relay coming up," he said.

"Yes," I said puzzled.

"Do you need someone to do the run?" he asked.

In many of the triathlons, the challenged athlete would take one leg of the race—their strongest—and have teammates take the other. One person does the swim, another does the bike, and one more person for the run. Rudy had a steady team. Robin Williams (yes, the actor) would take his bike leg, and Scott Tinley, whose wife was one of the founders of CAF, would run the marathon leg of the race. He had that team for every race for years. For me, my teammates changed each race.

My dad said he had been working out and wanted to run the marathon in my next race, if I would have him.

"If you need a teammate, I want to do it," he said.

The event was a half Ironman at La Jolla Cove in San Diego. It was a 1.2-mile swim, a fifty-six-mile bike, and a 13.1-mile run. We ended up having a whole year to prepare because there was a wildfire around the original date of the event. In that year, he started being more present in my life, calling to check on me, and sometimes we would see one another to train if I had a competition in DC. At fourteen I didn't feel like I needed a belated father figure, even if that father figure was my real-life dad. But I appreciated that he was making an effort to join me in my interests, which was nice.

My dad showed up to pick me up from my hotel around six in the morning looking like he was training for a body-building competition. He really had been working out. He was solid. We arrived at La Jolla Cove at 6:30. They had coffee and bagels and fruit for the racers. As the event kicked off, it was time for the national anthem. Samuel Nehemiah, a wheelchair user, belted out "The Starred-Spangled Banner" with his amazing operatic voice. He sang the national anthem every year, and I loved it each time. When Sam sang, you knew we were ready to race.

After the anthem, all the participants were led to their areas. I headed to the cove for the swim. I was one of the first to finish—in thirty-five minutes—and I could tell my dad was impressed.

We had a couple of hours to kill before my dad's run, so we checked out the vendors and walked around the beautiful cove. As the time got near, I could tell my dad was a little nervous. He didn't want to let me down. The tables had turned. I was in my element here. I was good, and with my sleeveless shirt, I looked like an athlete. I *was* a professional athlete.

Our bike leg was lagging. Since my team changed each year, I don't remember who did the bike leg, but I remember that by the time he came in, my dad would have to make up a lot of ground if we were going to win. And this course was not something he was prepared for. He had trained in Las Vegas, which had very few hills and valleys. This race was hilly and tough, so he struggled. He finished, but we didn't place.

It was great to see how much respect he had for what I was doing. "You inspire me!" he told me after the race. He said when he thinks about quitting or when things get tough, he often thinks about me and all that I do, and he pushes through. I think sometimes about what my life would have been had my dad been around. Would I be who I am? Or would he have been a crutch?

Things work out the way they are supposed to. Maybe if I didn't have to figure things out on my own, I wouldn't be this strong today. Maybe I wouldn't be so independent. Maybe I wouldn't have the confidence that I have.

———

I was getting back into the swing of things athletically, but my school situation was going in the wrong direction. I was attending Fairfield High Prep, which I loved. I met some good people there. But my grades were falling behind—again. I was coasting. I was more interested in training, hanging out, and playing video games than homework and studying. I knew I could do the work, I just didn't feel like doing it.

My mom talked with Alan and Alison about it, and once again they came through. They worked their magic and got me a scholarship to attend John Carroll Catholic High School in Birmingham, one of the best schools in the state of Alabama. It was also less than a mile away from Lakeshore—on the exact same block in fact. I started there the second semester of my sophomore year there and realized on day one that I was not going to be able to breeze through these classes.

In my first-period math class—a subject I was very good in—they used the exact same textbook that I was using at Fairfield High. We were on chapter 2 at the time I transferred. This class was on chapter 10! How were they so far ahead? I was lost. And the teacher, who was very good, saw I was having a hard time. At the same time, she was struggling to teach the class and catch me up. I met with her after class and she suggested a tutor, which I gladly accepted. I had tutors for just about every subject—I was that far behind. I was angry at Fairfield and at myself. I hadn't realized how much my casual approach to school had set me back. This school was a real challenge. I actually felt bad for all the smart kids at Fairfield High. They were not getting a good education. It was night and day. Fairfield was all Black and had a 60 percent dropout rate. But true to my competitive nature, I was determined to catch up and do well at Carroll.

At Fairfield, I knew I could pass everything with ease, I was just lazy. I had developed some bad habits, too—like not finishing my homework. One night, I went to bed and made the mistake of leaving my unfinished homework out on the kitchen table. It had to be about one in the morning when my mother stormed into my room and dragged me out of bed.

"You must be out of your mind!" she yelled (something she rarely did). "You *will* finish this homework tonight! And I will make sure you finish every night after this! You will not go to bed until you do."

I didn't get back to bed until two in the morning, but I made sure that my homework was done every night after that. I would not be dragged out of bed like that again. It was important that I graduate high school—something my mom hadn't done. So it made sense that she really cracked down on me. I needed that because the classes at this new school was so much harder.

My junior year in high school was perhaps my most challenging year. We moved again, this time to Hoover, Alabama. Hoover was closer to John Carroll and Lakeshore, and I joined the Hoover Swim Club. I was very busy keeping up with my studies and now two swim clubs. Alan spoke with the coach at Hoover and convinced him to let me swim with his team so I could advance in my training. He was not feeling the idea of having a double-amputee on his team. He seemed wary and unsure. The Hoover team was ranked in the state, and he was paid to make sure these kids got scholarships. But when he met me, he decided to let me try.

"You will swim in the open lanes," he told me. "If you can keep up, I'll let you swim with the team." I thought this was messed up at first, like I was being singled out. But I eventually understood.

I couldn't keep up with my teammates at first. At first, it was strange trying to swim and stay straight and not get in anyone's way. The pool was divided into six lanes—they had two fast lanes for the good swimmers, two lanes for those swimmers who were still getting it together, two lanes that were open to the public, where I was swimming.

The team trained with five or six swimmers per lane, and you had to swim in tandem, in a circle, for safety. I was having trouble just doing laps. I would end up veering into the lane next to mine, and quite a few times, the swimmer in my lane would catch up to me and lap me. I worked on my drills that Alan taught me and my technique—especially my backstroke, where swimmers would have to stay out of my way or get hit with a flying arm. I was ping-ponging all over that pool. But within three months of training, I had graduated out of the "public" lanes into the team lanes. I was with the slower swimmers, but I was officially with the team. I could keep up, but barely. The Hoover coach, seeing my progress, also helped me refine my stroke. Soon, I was one of the middle-of-the-pack swimmers on the team. I wasn't the fastest, but I also wasn't the slowest anymore.

I was rising in my sport. I was competing in meets with abled swimmers and finishing strong in the middle. I was even invited to the 2008 Paralympic Games in Beijing, China. I got a grant to go and watch through the Paralympic Academy with the hopes of competing in 2012.

Beijing was amazing. Not only did I get to see the Great Wall of China, but I pulled myself up the steps to experience this beautiful country.

The opening ceremonies were inspiring, with individuals with disabilities from around the world. People like my friend Rudy were there competing on an elite level. Watching them, I decided right there to train for the Paralympics with all my heart and full conviction. When I got home from Beijing, I told Alan, "I'm taking swimming more seriously!" I started doing double workouts with the Hoover swim team.

I even got to attend a prestigious camp in Colorado Springs. I had to fill out paperwork and write an essay on why I should be accepted.

There was a lot of talk about college around this time too. What were my options? There were applications to fill out and tests to take. My grades were now heading in the right direction, but I had to keep them up while training and traveling. I was under a lot of pressure. I was overwhelmed.

We were now living in the projects in Hoover, Alabama. It was nicknamed Guadalajara because there were a lot of neighbors from Central and South Americans in the area. Contractors would ride through in the mornings in trucks and looking for labor on the corners. Four or five guys would jump in the back of a pick-up truck for work.

We had a two-bedroom apartment that was teaming with roaches. In Fairfield, we had an occasional huge water bug. This place had the small, medium, and large variety of roaches, and they were everywhere. One morning, I was trying to work on my scholarship essay at the kitchen table, and a roach crawled across my paper. I just lost it.

Why can't things be normal?!

It was a question that was burning inside. On this one particular day, my feelings bubbled over, and I lashed out at my mom. She was at the kitchen sink, and she asked me to take the garbage to the dumpster. I had no problem doing chores. We often worked together to keep things running smoothly at the apartment. But the condition of this particular place, coupled with everything I was storing up—all the resentment, my expired patience, and a growing need for stability that seemed impossible—just came rushing to the surface.

"Why are we living like this?!" I yelled. "Why are we always living like this!"

I rarely raised my voice—especially to my mom. But I was simply fed up.

She stopped in her tracks and looked at me in a way I hadn't seen before. Then, she slowly turned and walked into the other room. I could hear her crying. She didn't cry when we lost the house. She didn't cry when we lost the car. She didn't cry any of the times we were in the shelters. It caught me off guard. I was sorry immediately.

After I yelled at her, she didn't speak to me for a couple of days, nothing but the basics, "Did you finish your homework?" or "What time is practice over?" but no conversation at all. This was out of the ordinary because my mom talked to me about anything and everything. I was her sounding board. I tried to make up by leaving sticky notes around the house letting her know how much I appreciated her. I *was* so sorry. She was doing her best to make this place a home. She was doing *her* best.

The ice started to melt, and we went back to our routine. On Friday nights, we would go to the library and pick out movies. Then we would go get pizza. Friday movie nights were back on! *Dragonheart* with Sean Connery was one of our favorites. And I loved *The Fifth Element* with Bruce Willis and Chris Tucker. Our go-to movie, though, was, of course, *The Color Purple*, starring Whoopi Goldberg, Oprah Winfrey, and Danny Glover. My mom loved that movie. We had to have watched that film at least a dozen times. As time went on, I realized she loved it so much because she could see so much of herself and her upbringing in that film.

We were watching it yet again, and during the scene where Miss Celie was being violated, my mom casually said, "I know that feeling. My first time wasn't my choice, either." I was stunned. By that age I knew what rape was, but I never thought it could have happened to my mom.

That was all she said. I didn't ask any questions. We went back to watching.

She later told me her father (or the man who was with her mother at the time) raped her. I also know she had a cousin on her mother's side who was staying with them for a while who violated her. He was eighteen. He lured my ten-year-old mother into the woods just outside of camp and raped and beat her. She said Grandma did nothing, which is probably why their relationship was so fractured. The pieces were starting to form then, and I understood why my mother moved the way she did.

Mom would tell stories like this here and there, always told in a matter-of-fact way. With no emotion. No reflection. Just telling it as if she would tell me about her day. She held a lot in, and she needed to let it out in her own way, in her own time. I never pressured her for more. This was her way, and I understood. I'm amazed at my mother's resilience. Her ability to do what needs to be done, no matter what, despite having had so little herself.

Looking back, that day that I snapped, I had every right to do that. But I was also going through an immature, selfish phase. I was only concerned with what was going on with me. I didn't consider what my mother was going through. I also didn't consider her fears.

Her whole life had been figuring out ways to make sure I had the things I needed. And now I would be going away, not needing her as much. What would become of her? She never discussed that, but I know she was scared and thinking about it. Who was she without me?

This is a question, I believe, she is still grappling with.

And with big changes looming in my own life, I was asking the question of myself, too: Who am I?

Chapter Fourteen

COMING OF AGE

JASMINE LOOKED BEAUTIFUL IN HER LONG, RED OFF-THE-shoulder dress. I had on a black tuxedo, with a white shirt and a matching red tie and vest. My mom made sure I had a little wrist carnation to put on my date.

I was going to the prom!

We all met up at Tia's house. She lived in one of those homes you'd see on *MTV Cribs*. It even had an elevator.

"We're taking photos at your spot!" I told her in school the day before. Everyone's parents were there taking pictures. My mom was so proud.

The black stretch limo pulled up to get us from Tia's. And off we went. Me, Jasmine, and Tony and Tia—the rest of our John Carroll Catholic crew.

Jasmine was quiet and smart. And her mom, who was very protective, was okay with me taking her because she knew there would be no funny business. And she was right. Heck, I didn't even take my first drink until I was twenty-one . . . and that was with my mom to celebrate my birthday! I never smoked, never cut class, and I was a virgin.

Jasmine's mom and my mom were cool, too. They met at school events and struck up a friendship. There were only a handful of Black families at the mostly white John Carroll Catholic High School, and we all gravitated toward one another and formed a community.

Jasmine wasn't my girlfriend, which made the night even more fun. There was no pressure. We were a bunch of kids hanging out, laughing and dancing. Well, I wasn't much of a dancer. I could do a two-step and that was about it. I had great rhythm, thanks to my ancestry. But my prosthetic legs couldn't keep up with some of the more elaborate dances my friends were doing. We swag surfed, which was fun. And there was a line dance or two. I didn't get to slow dance at my prom, but I was happy to be there.

After prom, we went to a fancy restaurant. My mom had given me a hundred dollars from my disability check to pay for my and Jasmine's meal. I splurged and ordered a steak. This was the same group I ate with at school. The Black kids sat together in the cafeteria every day. We might have one or two cool white kids who would come and eat with us, but it was mostly just us. I never had a situation in San Diego where I felt so out of place because of my race. My schools were usually diverse. But I felt that way at CAF events in the South, especially the occasional trip to Texas. And at John Carroll Catholic. At school, it wasn't overt racism as much the loneliness from just being culturally and physically different.

It was important for me to be a "normal" kid—just like everybody else. And to have safe places where I could be myself and not have to feel watched or judged.

I learned how to drive the way a lot of kids my age learned—by taking driving lessons. Alabama Vocational Rehab had a class for disabled learners, which was free to me. They had a vehicle with hand controls. I play video games, so I was excited to get behind the wheel of a car and be in control. Getting my license would be one more thing that would make me feel like everyone else.

My mom had an old GMC Jimmy, and she would take me to a remote parking lot to practice. She had one of the neighborhood mechanics install hand controls for a couple hundred bucks. Not only did the hand breaks make the car useable for me; they also enabled my mom to put me on her insurance.

The hand controls were like a gear shift in a manual car. The foot of the shift had bars or levers that fit over the brake and the gas so that when I pushed forward on the shift, it would press down on the brake. When I pulled back on the rod, it would press down on the gas. What was cool was that the device could be folded in two when not in use. So my mom could drive without removing it. In some cases, she would just use my controls because it was so easy.

The hardest part about driving was learning how to parallel park. I still see abled people who struggle with parallel parking. That was tricky because I really had to manipulate the hand controls to back up and cut the wheel. There was a lot of pulling forward and backing up before I got the hang of it. Angles are the key to parallel parking. I eventually got it down and even learned how to drive with prosthetics on. It was definitely more difficult and a bit uncomfortable. But I could do it.

Rudy can manipulate his prosthetics so well that he drives without hand controls. I also have a friend who is visually impaired who drives! It's incredible. The technology today is amazing. His car has these features that can "see" for him and talks to him. The thing about being differently abled is that you often have to be more proficient and more careful than most, which can make you a better driver.

So in my senior year of high school, my mom let me drive to school. I had practice afterward. Mom worked the morning shift at Jacks, a fast-food restaurant in Hoover. We made a deal. She started at six in the morning. If I wanted to use the car, I would have to drop her off for her shift and pick her up and drop her off at home. Then I could have the car until after practice in the evening. That meant setting the alarm for 5 a.m., which I gladly did. On days when my mom needed the car, I would use Access-A-Ride to get to school or catch a ride with Leah, who also swam on the Hoover team.

On Sundays, I would go to church—something I hadn't done much in San Diego. We started going when we moved in with Grandma Rozell. She was a staunch churchgoer, and her church was strict. They didn't believe in having music. There was no organ or drums or anything. We sang from the hymn book a cappella. There was no screaming and shouting—just the Scripture and the sermon. My mom liked it. I didn't, at first, but by the time I started high school, I was reading the scripture for the sermon and leading prayer.

When we moved to Hoover, I started going to a nondenominational church in the area. I was invited by Hasaan, who I met at a CAF event the previous year at their annual fundraiser. He was a baseball player. He was a few grades behind me, and I became his mentor. I was to him what Rudy was to me.

Hasaan was an incredible athlete. I had never seen anyone master the prosthetics with the mechanical knee the way he had. The knee was very funky. You had to land on your heel just right or you would end up on your behind. I barely could walk when I had mine, let alone run a baseball field. But Hasaan could not only hit; he could also take off running. To this day, I have never seen anyone run in the kind of prosthetic he had and not fall. It was mind blowing. So was his church. It had the full band and choir, and I really enjoyed Sunday service there.

Senior year of high school was going amazing. My cousin Brittney moved to Alabama to be with her mom—my mother's baby sister. After years of struggling, she was finally on her feet, and Brittney wanted to be with her. I think she missed me too, since we'd been so close as kids.

That year, I was featured in *USA Today*. There was an article about the high percentage of Black children who don't know how to swim. The article featured Alison and a picture of her training me. When I got to school that morning, everyone was passing around copies of the newspaper and patting me on the back. I was a mini-celebrity after that.

"You do know this article is *not* about me, right?" I told my friends. But they didn't care. I was in the paper!

Things were getting better for me. My mom and I moved from the roach-infested projects to a decent apartment complex in Hoover. My grades were getting better and better, and so was my swimming. I was able to shave a full thirty seconds off my 200-meter freestyle time. That was unheard of for someone my age. Small children can take those leaps, but not teens. Training with the Hoover Swim Club was paying off.

And I was graduating! This was bittersweet for my mom. Me going to college not only meant me leaving her alone. It also meant that my disability assistance would be stopping, too. She had spent so much of our lives managing that check as the major source of income and filling in the rest working at low-paying jobs. Her whole life had been about me and my needs. Now she would have to learn how to focus on herself.

I could feel her fear and sadness. And also, her joy. She had gotten me over one of the biggest hurdles thus far—putting me through school. She bought me my cap and gown. She felt bad that she could only afford a basic package instead of the one with the class ring.

"One day, I'll get one if I want it," I told her. "It's no big deal, really." I never did get the ring because it wasn't important. What was important: graduating.

Chapter Fifteen

BMOC (BLACK MAN ON CAMPUS)

I WAS ACCEPTED TO TWO SCHOOLS—THE UNIVERSITY OF NORTH Alabama and Troy University. Troy didn't have a swim team, so the choice was easy.

Before I officially accepted the offer at the University of North Alabama, I visited the campus. It was in Florence, which was a couple of hours from where I lived. Alan called ahead and connected with the swim coach, "My kid is coming to check out the school. Look out for him."

I met the coach. I met the swimmers. They were all very nice. I let them know I was looking forward to training with them. Some of them looked skeptical. They had never seen a double amputee swim, let alone compete at their level. But once I got in the water, all doubt faded. I was one of the best on the team in my best stroke—the breaststroke.

Getting me into John Carroll Catholic and on the Hoover Swim

Club altered my future for the better. And I owe all of that to Alison and Alan! Because of them, I was the first in my immediate family to go to a four-year college. And now I would be competing on a college level and possibly the Paralympics, which was the goal. I did the work, too—getting an academic scholarship to go along with the financial aid I was offered.

Leaving my mom was going to be difficult for both of us, but I knew I had to.

College was a major adjustment. For the first time in my life, I was on my own. My dorm room was in LaGrange, a six-floor building in the middle of campus. My room was on the first floor. It was a typical room with two beds—one on each side of the room, two desks, and two closets. I had my own closet, with not much to put in it. My mom scraped together enough money to send me off with sheets and toiletries, but I didn't have much else. I was first to arrive. My roommate, who was from the area, didn't show up until a day before school started, so I had the room to myself for a week. I had time to adjust to this new reality.

LaGrange Hall was coed. Another adjustment. The men were on one side of the hallway, women on the other side. We were separated by the entrance. The resident assistant, the RA, was a woman. She stayed in a big room in the middle. There was an elevator in front of the entrance, and our bathroom was all the way down the hall from my room.

I thought, "Oh man, I have to walk all the way down this hall in my towel every day?!"

I would wear my stubbies, my short prosthetics, to the showers. I slide them onto my stumps like house shoes. They are more convenient because I can just slide them on and off. They reminded me of the days of the Tupperware cups—just more official and fitted. I used stubbies when we lived in the shelters, so that my bare stumps wouldn't touch the floors.

Each morning, I shuffled down the hall in my stubbies looking like a penguin from *Happy Feet*. I was a spectacle, and my hallmates couldn't help but stare. I mean, I was a sight in my stubbies with my towel around my waist practically dragging along the floor. I was also a sight from the waist up. My upper body was solid. I was in the best shape of my life.

I heard a guy say something like, "Man, he looks strong," as I shuffled by. I was proud of my body. And I was flaunting it. There was a handicapped shower, which had a bench. Everyone liked using my shower (they called it *my* shower because I was the only handicapped person in the whole dorm). It had the hottest water. Everyone made sure I took my shower before using it. I never had to wait. But after I took my shower everyone else would fight over it.

Bobby, my roommate, showed up on a Sunday. I was happy and relieved when I saw him. "Cool, you're Black!" he said when we met. There were only three Black dudes in our dorm...and two of them were in *this* room. We rested easy.

Bubby, who was getting a degree in criminal justice to become a detective, was from a town about an hour outside of Florence, Alabama. He was used to the culture. I still was adjusting, even after years.

I had the TV and PS3, which he was happy about. He brought the small refrigerator, which I was happy about. That first year we were each other's safe haven. He lived just an hour away and could go home every weekend if he wanted, but he stayed and we hung out. He made my transition so much easier. I needed that friend. There were also Taylor and Evan, who stayed on the floor above us. And Anaya. She stayed across campus in an all-women's dorm. I met her in the cafeteria—one of my favorite places.

The cafeteria is where the social butterfly in me came out. I guess food was a good motivator. I would see Anaya and Mariana eating by themselves sometimes, so I went over and introduced myself and ate with them one day. We became really close that year.

I adjusted rather quickly to college life. I'd learned to wash clothes at an early age and did my laundry every week. My mom and I would be in the laundromat every weekend. Bubby and I kept our room nice—so nice that our friends would hang out in our room. We had a real community.

This is dope! I thought to myself after I settled in. I was enjoying my freshman year.

I had my sights on joining Alpha Phi Alpha, the frat of W. E. B. Du Bois, Paul Robeson, and Martin Luther King Jr. But when I found out how much it cost to pledge, I had to pass on all of it. I barely had enough money for food. Instead, I focused on training and graduating. And Anaya.

Anaya was the quintessential Southern belle. When you think of Southern hospitality, that's Anaya. She hung out with three other women—all smart and beautiful. I would see her on campus and think, *She's out of my league!* But our paths kept crossing. We would have classes together. We would eat together in the cafeteria every day. But we were just friendly—nothing romantic at first. I couldn't imagine her wanting to go out with me.

I was confident in most areas, but I was self-conscious, too.

I had never approached a woman. I was too shy. I never thought anyone would want me. My mom would tell me how handsome I was, but who believes their mom?

As early as I can remember, my mother would instill confidence in me through positive affirmations. When we had the house, she used to stand me in front of the mirror in her bedroom and make me look at myself. I hated looking in the mirror, but she would hold me in front of it.

"Look how handsome you are," she would say.

When I was two years old, she bought me a tuxedo and we went out to dinner. She wanted me to feel special. And I did. My mother constantly told me how handsome I was and how smart I was. But she's supposed to say those things, right?

In high school, I had a huge crush on Tatyana Ali from *Fresh Prince of Bel Air*. If I imagined a girlfriend, she would be like Ashley Banks. Anaya, though, was very close and very real. We connected over spiritual discussions and church. And the more we talked, the more I liked her. I worked up the courage to ask her on a date. I saved up my money and invited her to dinner at Applebee's.

"What took you so long?!" she asked as we ate a basket of chicken tenders.

"I thought you were out of my league," I said. I mean...look at you!" Anaya was five-foot-five with mocha-colored skin and curves for days.

She shook her head and said, "Look at *you*!"

I learned that despite what you hear, most women care more about your character than your looks—most good women. I learned a lot about myself being with Anaya. With her, there was no pressure to be anything more than who I was. And she encouraged me to become even more of myself. And I think being with me also offered her some ease, too.

I was still a virgin. And everyone knew it because I was very open about it. I'd had a girlfriend for two weeks in high school in my junior year. We held hands and we kissed once. I wasn't experienced at all. Heck, this date with Anaya was my first real date.

We hung out for the rest of the semester, and it was nice. For a while, we were *that* couple on campus—always together. Until summer break. That's when we seemed to take a break, too.

Sophomore year, I met Sally. She approached me on campus and struck up a conversation. She would drop in on me at my dorm room. I was disappointed when she told me she had a boyfriend who was about ten years older than she was. But she also told me that she liked me. *Liked me–liked me.* One night we were hanging out in my room. My roommate was home for the weekend, and Sally and I started kissing.

"I want to be your first," she told me.

I wanted my first time to be right. And internally, I knew being with Sally would be wrong. Besides, she had a boyfriend! And with that came a whole lot of drama. He called me (I don't know how he got my number) and said he wanted to fight me when he heard that she and I were hanging out. I told him I wasn't going to fight him. We squashed it on the phone. But after that, I was done with Sally, no drama.

Later that semester, I met Anaya. She thought I was funny. We bonded over music—old R&B like Tony Terry. She was easy to talk with, so we talked, about everything and nothing at all until the wee hours of the morning.

"I know you're proud of being a virgin," she said. "So am I."

What a great relief. We could go at our own pace. And we did.

Sex was *nothing* like I had imagined. It was nothing like in the movies. It was painful for her, which was confusing for me. I didn't know what I was supposed to do with my body. And I had the added struggles with having prosthetics.

I had all the wrong impressions. And so much anxiety, too. My first time wasn't great for either of us. And I had no one to talk to about it. I couldn't talk to my roommate or friends because I didn't want them running their mouths. But I figured it out and learned—as I did everything. I learned that sex was more about discovering each other's likes and dislikes. It's about being attentive, trying different things, and seeing what feels good.

It took me about a whole year to get comfortable, comfortable being intimate and comfortable with my body. Anaya helped me a lot with that. She helped me love myself. I was still struggling with my complexion. I had my whole life. But Anaya loved my skin. Yes, my mom would tell me I was handsome. And my aunts. And older ladies in the church. But there's nothing like getting attention from women who aren't your family! And I never really got that in San Diego.

In Alabama, in that southern sun, I was extra dark. I have heard all the jokes like, "Man, you must sweat oil." I have been called "midnight." I would walk into every room and notice that I was the darkest person. I would actually look around to see if I was. I was more self-conscious about my skin tone than my disability.

But Anaya loved my complexion.

"You're so beautiful," she would tell me as she caressed my face. I was starting to believe her.

It was what I needed, and it carried over into all parts of my life. I was already confident competing, but this relationship gave me a little more.

———

I don't know which was the bigger challenge to overcome... being a dark-skinned Black man or a double amputee.

The older I get, the more I'm aware of how my Blackness is seen in the United States and some other parts of the world. I spent most of my life navigating my disabilities and having people stare at me or treat me differently because I was the boy with no legs.

I was sixteen when I realized that for some, seeing a Black person may be the bigger deal for people. I was competing in one of my first Paralympic swim competitions with CAF outside of California. They had flown me to Waco, Texas, for the event and I was excited. I had never been to Texas.

I had gotten there early, and I was walking around the venue looking at other matches when I noticed all eyes were on me. I thought, *This is strange*. I mean it couldn't be that I was walking around on prosthetics. This was a *Paralympic* event. Everyone there had some type of disability. And there were literally prosthetic legs scattered around everywhere.

For a second, I wondered whether my name had gotten around because I was on a winning streak. But then I realized that some of the looks were menacing. Others turned up their noses when they saw me. I didn't understand why I was getting these looks, and dirty looks, at that. Rudy was there, which was a relief—a friendly face.

"What's up with the looks I'm getting?" I asked him. I could tell he noticed.

"You are the first Black person many of these people have ever been around," he said to me, matter-of-factly. Rudy is Mexican but looks white. And he was a superstar in the Paralympic community. So he was the exception—like so many professional superstar athletes in baseball, football, and basketball. Even the most hardened racist would want Michael Jordan's or Ken Griffey Jr.'s or even Herschel Walker's autograph and a picture. But I was some random kid at this event. They didn't know me. All they knew was that I was Black.

I had experienced racism before. My mom and I once stayed in Lakeside, a part of San Diego where Black people didn't live, but it was one of the only places we could afford. It was mostly occupied by poor whites and us. One night we were walking home. There were no sidewalks, so we were close to the side of the road when a guy in a truck came bearing down on us, missing us by inches. I don't know if he was trying to hit us or scare us, but he came so close and swerved at the last minute and ended up in somebody's yard. My mom stopped.

"Let's wait for him to leave," she said. "We don't know if he intends to harm us."

"Mama, why would he want to harm us?" I asked.

"Baby, some people are just hateful," she said.

California was tricky. You didn't know where racism would pop up. And you also had to be concerned with the police. I took the bus most of my life, so we had very few encounters with the police. With Alabama came a different brand of racism. You knew what you were dealing with in Alabama because it was more of a general atmosphere, despite having less exposure to Black people. And because we lived in the Black part of Alabama, there wasn't much interaction for racism to rear its head.

In Texas was the first time I experienced actual racism. And it was in a place where I never expected it. The disabled community is pretty tight knit and friendly. I mean we are dealing with different disabilities. Who has time to be racist? Apparently, these disabled Texans!

I was shocked. *How in the world is this possible?*

It's not that I wasn't aware of my color. I was. Growing up, Black people, mostly older Black women would come up to me and say, "Oh, what a handsome chocolate baby!" or "You're such a cute little dark-skinned boy." The adults always showered me with those comments.

The children, however, would say, "You're so *BLACK*!" in a negative way.

There was one year, the fourth grade, when the teasing was brutal. My reaction to it wasn't the best. Remember how I handled the little boy who stomped on my stump? Well, I would put my hands on anyone who teased me, too. I developed a bit of a reputation. The kids knew that if they made fun of me, I might bop them in the mouth. So the teasing stopped. I was dealing with instability and living in shelters; I wasn't going to tolerate being bullied at school on top of that.

There was one kid in particular who kept calling me "Blackie" and things like that. We were at lunch, and he was holding court running his mouth, and I went up to him and socked him as hard as I could. I know it hurt because he stopped. I knew I couldn't take on everyone, but I tried. By the fifth grade, everyone knew not to chance it.

Getting the kids to stop teasing me didn't change how I felt about myself though. I trusted what my peers were saying more than my mother and the women in my village. For a while, I hated how I looked. I *was* so Black, *and* I didn't have legs.

When my mother stood me in front of the mirror and made me look at myself and call me handsome, I hated it. I hated how I looked because I knew I was different. When I became a teenager, I became even more self-conscious when it came to girls. *Would a girl ever like me? Would I have a girlfriend?*

Those questions were answered, of course, in the nicest of ways. And much of my insecurities fell away, replaced by a quiet confidence that bordered on cockiness. I had friends. I was popular. My vision of myself, however, had to catch up with my popularity.

Excelling in competitive sports has made me stand out in a good way. It has made people want to get to know me. I have only known myself as an amputee, so that was never something for me to focus on. In fact, I'm more comfortable without my prosthetics. I feel more me when I'm getting around on my stumps. The prosthetics make me feel strange . . . like I don't belong to me.

But me, butt naked, no prosthetics, stumps out, I'm fine!

I believe it's important for my face to be seen. I know if Rudy had turned down that engagement that day and I never saw him, I probably wouldn't be where I am today. So much of our conversations center on representation, but it's more about inspiration. If you can see a thing, you can be a thing. I know there is a little boy or girl in the Paralympic world who needs to connect with me. Seeing someone like me, who looks like me, can open up the possibilities for so many young people about what *they* can do.

Standing among all the booths and advertisements and promises of everything Paralympians could do, I knew I wanted to compete seriously—*really* seriously—at the Ironman World Championship. I wouldn't be racing for myself. I would become the first above-the-knee double amputee to finish. But I would also be the first *Black* above-the-knee amputee to do so. That was just as important to me.

Chapter Sixteen

THE SECOND LEG: THE BIKE

IT WAS NINETY-EIGHT DEGREES. AND THE SUN WAS BEATING down on me in a way I hadn't expected.

Growing up in San Diego, the temperatures often reach the high 90s, but this seemed hotter, more humid, and more oppressive. I heard it was even worse in previous years at the Ironman in Kona and as hot as 104 degrees one year. I couldn't imagine that at all. This was going to be one of the most challenging things I had ever done. And I wasn't prepared.

This was the second leg of the Ironman race—112 miles of open road. I'd spent much of the first leg of the race in the dark, chilly water. But now the sun was fully out and shining.

I made my way to the transition area, wrapped a towel around my waist, and changed into my biking shorts and shirt. I grabbed my handcycle, which, at five feet long, was bigger than I was. I took a deep breath and readied myself for what would be the hardest leg of this race for me. If the swim was my best event, the bike would be my worst. One hundred and twelve miles would be difficult for a person with both legs, but for adaptive athletes, the bike is a make-or-break event.

It was a break for Rudy. Several years before me, he made an attempt to become the first above-the-knee double amputee to complete this Ironman race in Kona. It was the bike portion that did him in. To be named a champion, each leg has to be completed in a certain amount of time, and the entire race has to be done in seventeen hours. Rudy missed the bike cutoff by fifteen minutes. He rode a standard stand-up bicycle using his prosthetics instead of a handcycle or other adaptive bike. About fifty miles in, his back seized up. He pushed through that, but by the end, his stumps were so raw, the pain was unbearable.

I tried training on a traditional stationary bike in the gym. But it didn't take me long to see how that wasn't going to work for me. My prosthetics pinched and rubbed my stumps within the first mile, and I could see how Rudy's back seized up on him. Handcycle it was! The handcycle allowed me to use my greatest strength—my arms. But it, too, had its challenges.

I got the bike I was using for this race from CAF three months earlier. That's how much training time I had. Two weeks prior to coming to Kona, I did my first individual half-triathlon in Montauk, New York—no relay. I *struggled* to finish because of the bike leg. So I was super nervous about it here. I initially thought that doing a race three months before the world championship would clear me of my jitters. It did just the opposite.

Not only was I unsure whether I would finish the Ironman in Kona; my body had not fully recovered. I was still blistered and sore. That horrible half-triathlon took a lot out of me. I left Montauk feeling anything but confident. I was hurting after completing a *half* Ironman, how in the world would I finish a full one . . . and in two weeks?!

This was real—double the distance and double the heat.

After finishing my race in Montauk, I gingerly walked back to my car on tender limbs. I drove to a local bar and had a celebratory burger. While it wasn't pretty, I *did* finish. And I *always* celebrated the finishes.

Over the following two weeks leading to the Ironman in Kona, I focused on core work, mainly sit-ups, which would help me in the swim and bike. I stretched diligently. I even meditated, something I had just started doing. I also started a new morning routine while brushing my teeth. I would stop brushing and look at myself in the mirror. I would stare, take a deep breath and smile. As I forced myself to smile, the act itself made me laugh and my smile grew wider. As I was looking in the mirror back at a joyful me, I began visualizing bouncing across the finish line in my running blades at the Ironman. I imagined the cheering crowd waiting for me at the finish line. I saw my mom. Arms open, waiting to hug me. My arms are in the air and I'm smiling ear to ear as she wraps her arms around me and the crowd is cheering harder.

You can do it! I'd tell myself.

Nobody had done it. Not even Rudy. I was here because of Rudy. He always set the bar and allowed for me to see the possibilities.

He was a sounding board when I had doubts and an extinguisher, making sure those doubts never inflamed. I was going to finish what he started in Kona.

Forget the heat. Forget my still-tender stumps. Forget the poor finish in New York. I was going to finish here! So I grabbed my bike. The small compartment of my cycle is a sort of cockpit with enough room for my bottom, my stumps, a couple of bottles of water, and some food. I would eat periodically during the race for energy—a few bananas, a couple of peanut butter and jelly sandwiches, and some Vega protein bars. I'd had a little bit of black coffee before the swim, and boy was I hungry! I ate one banana, put on my biking gloves, got in the cockpit of my bike, and started on my way.

As I made my way to the starting line, I saw other competitors chatting and socializing. I was off to myself. I had no time to waste. One hundred and twelve miles were waiting for me. I decided I would tackle it the way I do everything—head on, dealing with what was right and front of me. I needed to finish the bike in ten hours and thirty minutes and the entire race in under seventeen, or else I would be disqualified. I just had to keep pushing.

The hand cycle is great because it allows me to sit. The hand cycle is also horrible because although I can sit for hours and hours, I am solely relying on my arms. One hundred and twelve miles of an arm workout? And I had only three months to train for that! Some amputees can use a standup bike comfortably using prosthetics. But the prosthetics for me are awkward and eventually become very painful, like they had for Rudy. While training with the hand cycle, the only issue I experienced was my back tightening. But that was after only 20 to 30 miles, not 112.

This bike leg had to be near perfect—meaning no flat tires, and definitely no accidents, which happens during these races. I knew I wasn't going to be fast, but I needed to be solid. Slow and steady wins the race, right?

The first nine miles were smooth. I had time to appreciate some of the beauty I'd glimpsed when I emerged from the ocean: the palm trees, the blue sky with its billowy clouds spread out, the ocean with its crashing waves. It was beautiful and chaotic as the abled bikers crowded the road to grab their place in this race.

Around mile 10, an incident occurred. Someone clipped my back wheel. I ride low to the ground so if you're not paying attention on a traditional bike, you could easily miss me. But being low to the ground also has its advantages. It's more difficult for me to topple over. I dipped, swerved, and kept going. I kept seeing swimmers entering the bike portion. The first para-athlete passed me around mile 7, and several more had passed me by the time I got to mile 10. All were single-limb amputees (either arm or leg). Still, I knew there were still people finishing the swim leg and entering the road for the bike. By this time, all the professional men and women were ahead of me, but now quite a few amateurs were also passing me by.

I saw a bunch of them drop out, however, around mile 20. This was hard for everyone.

About thirty-five miles in, I got nauseous and started vomiting. I had listened to other racers who recommended that I eat every fifteen to twenty minutes. I had never done a race like this before, so while it didn't seem to make sense, I did it anyway. I had that banana before I started and then ate a sandwich and an energy bar during the first hour. My body didn't agree with that schedule. Combined with the intense physicality and the heat, I was toast.

The purge, however, was a blessing. I felt so much better after throwing up twice. I was able to get back in rhythm.

In the swim, I had my technique to pull me through when my mind was spinning. In this bike leg, it was just the opposite. Those meditation techniques and visualizations that I practiced were a savior. I was able to zone out and focus on my breathing and pedaling. I picked up the pace and started passing people.

Around mile 50 came the winds. It was blowing about twenty-five miles per hour and higher. That's why the water was so choppy. The heat and the wind were a vicious combination. But my bike was longer than a traditional bike, and low to the ground, so the wind didn't cut me as much as those on the stand-up bikes. It was still whipping my face and knocking the air out of me though.

I'd done a test ride of the course a couple of days before the actual race. It was a morning ride and there was no wind that early, just the beautiful rolling hills. I thought, *This isn't going to be so bad.* But it was that bad. The wind made those rolling hills scary. I hit a headwind so strong, it felt like I was cycling in place. Once I made it to halfway point, which was a loop that led back to the transition area, the wind changed. I thought, *Great! The wind will be at my back now.* Wrong! This thing was now hitting us sideways, blowing me toward the edge of the road.

That wind took out a lot of people. I heard about three women who got blown over by the gusts, which had gotten as high as forty miles an hour. They spun out and ran into each other. There were even pros who dropped out because of the wind. For me, winds blew in a second round of nausea.

The winds finally died down as I headed into the final forty miles. The nausea subsided and I was finally settled. This race was grueling. There were so many who had dropped out at this point and so many who kept going despite being sick and even injured.

Addi Zerrenner finished the Ironman having done number 2 three times during the race. She said, "I'm not going to drop out with sh*t all over me. I'm going to finish with sh*t all over me!" And she did. The twenty-five-year-old running coach and personal trainer came in thirtieth place.

Soiling yourself during an Iron Man is a common occurrence. People don't stop to go to the bathroom; it takes too much precious time. I'm grateful that I didn't have to, but it's very common, especially in the last leg. Racers, real competitors, won't let anything stop them—not even diarrhea.

I know of racers who have left the course on stretchers. That was the only way I was stopping. I would have to be unconscious. I would rather give my all and have them forcibly remove me from the race than quit.

By mile 75, I had hit my stride. I even took a moment to enjoy the ride. The scenery of this race is almost indescribable. The sky, the water. You could see all the little islands surrounding Kona from our biking route. Hawaii is just beautiful. I could get lost in the coastline. San Diego's beaches were nice, but Hawaii is in a league of its own—just breathtaking.

With the wind, the heat, the nausea, and the worst of the fatigue behind me, I allowed myself to take in the beauty. I focused on this amazing view that few ever get to see. I could see Mauna Kea, the tallest peak in Hawaii, on the horizon. Mauna Kea almost kept me out of the race. There were protests stemming from the thirty-meter telescope proposed on the site. Protesters, who call themselves *kia'i*, or "protectors," argued that the construction of the telescope would further desecrate Mauna Kea, which is already home to about a dozen telescopes. I was down for the protest. I also learned about their Black king David. David Kalākaua was the last king of Hawaii, who ruled from 1874 to 1891. In fact, when white Southerners settled the Hawaiian Islands in the 1800s, they had a song about the Native people. The lyrics were said to be, "You may call them Hawaiian, but they look like n*ggers to me...." That, and the lengths that Hawaiians went to protect their land, resonated with me—I knew what it was like to have a home taken from you. I also knew my training and dreams had brought me here, and that if King David could be a leader, I could be a winner, too.

I was grateful to be able to experience all of this, being who I am.

By mile 90, I caught my third wind. I was in the zone for the next stretch. There were racers all around me, most on regular racing bicycles. Along the route, people were cheering us on. This was a definite departure from the solitude of training, where it is just me, the bike, and the road. I didn't know how much I needed the encouragement of others until that day. My mom was always there with a "you can do it!" and "you got this!" I knew she would be waiting for me at the finish line, and I had to get to her.

In the last seven miles, my body started to break down. My fingers were cramping. My arms, which were on fire, had all but burned out. I couldn't quit, though. Five more miles. Four more miles. Three more miles. Two...They inched by until I had one mile to go. *I got this.*

Exhausted, thirsty, and almost mentally defeated, I wheeled into the transition area at around 3:30 in the afternoon. I finished this leg! It took nine hours. I had sores on my bottom from the chafing. I couldn't feel my fingers. My stumps were raw. The muscles in my arms were beyond spent. But I finished!

I dragged myself to the changing area to find my running legs.

Chapter Seventeen

FLOWS AND EBBS

DURING THE HOLIDAYS AND THE SUMMER BREAKS, I WOULD GO back to San Diego to train with Alan and Alison. My goal was to qualify for my first national team. I had done endurance work with my swim team in Alabama. But the refinement, drills, and discipline that I needed to be a true athlete could only happen with Alan and Alison.

They had their first baby when I was leaving for college. Her name was Malia, like Barack and Michelle Obama's daughter. She was adorable, and I considered her another one of my sisters. And she loved me, too. They brought her to every competition. She turned into one of the best cheerleaders any athlete could want.

I was competing to make the national team for the SB6. Each class and event had a letter and a number to identify the event and the level of competition. The numbers represented the severity of the disability of the competitor. The lower the number, the more severe the disability. We were no longer competing in age groups. So SB6 stood for swim breaststroke, level 6. When I competed in the freestyle, I was an S8, which is mostly upper body strength, because I had a strong upper body. The breast-stroke requires a lot of kick. And without legs, I would be disad-vantaged swimming against swimmers with one leg or both legs and no arms. But despite the severity of my disability, I knew I had the skill on lock.

I was set to compete in the SB6 category for Team USA at the para-swimming event in Minneapolis, Minnesota, to determine whether I would make the national team. I finished in 1:37, which was a good time. I wouldn't find out whether I actually made the squad for another week when the other events taking place throughout the country finished.

I got the call on April 29, 2014. My birthday! I qualified. I also had pneumonia.

While I was preparing for the race, my school's pool was shut down for cleaning. So was the pool where the swim team met in Hoover. I found a pool that I knew was sketchy. It wasn't very clean, but I was focused on training and couldn't afford a break in my schedule. The dirty pool, plus the cold weather, coupled with my too-cool attitude about wearing a hat and scarf landed me with a serious bout of pneumonia. It was horrible.

I was hardly ever sick, and now I was so sick that I missed my school's Spring Fling. Ludacris was performing, and I'd really wanted to see him. But I made the national team. Silver lining!

When I recovered, I was back to training. I didn't want to just make the national team; I wanted to win. I had five months to prepare. In between finding out that I made the team and the tune-up international meet in Pasadena, I graduated from college.

I had taken a light load the last couple of semesters to make space for training. My major was communications. I had a case of senioritis—just like in high school, but I only had a couple of more classes to take to graduate. This time I *knew* I was going to graduate. And I was clear about where I was headed next.

My graduation was in December 2014.

My mom was there, of course. It was a two-hour drive, and she was there early helping me get ready. Alan came. Alison stayed back in San Diego with Malia. My grandma Rozell, my uncle Ray, and my cousin Rashad were there, too (Rahman had to work). My cousin Brittney was there. Besides my mom and later Alan and Alison, Brittney was always in my corner. Her mom, my auntie Freddy, was there with her husband and their daughter. My family rolled deep! My girlfriend, Anaya, was graduating, too, and her family was there in the crowd.

My high school graduation had been over the top, loud, and rowdy. There's even video of me walking across the stage for my diploma and the whole auditorium erupting in cheers. At the University of North Alabama, the state's oldest public university, there were strict rules about celebrating the graduates. No cheering. No whistling. No applause until everyone received their diploma. It was a quiet two-hour ceremony. And there was no celebratory dinner or anything afterward. Alan had to get back to California, and everyone else had a long drive back home.

But I was grateful they all came. And I was even more glad to be done.

I was the first in my family to get a degree from a four-year university. I had multiple cousins who had an associate's degree, and soon after, my sister Jonei went to college and finished with a master's degree in counseling. But I was the first with a four-year diploma. I was proud. My mother was especially proud. Once again, I fulfilled something she believed she was denied. She was living vicariously through me.

After graduation, I moved back to San Diego. My mom stayed in Alabama.

I had to take my training to the next level if I was going to make the national team and eventually the Olympics. When I moved, Anaya and I broke up. The long-distance relationship wasn't working for either of us. And she was a traditional church girl who wanted to be courted and married sooner than later.

"I'm not moving across the country for a man who isn't my husband," she told me. And I completely understood. But I knew at twenty-one, I wasn't ready to be married. And I told her that neither was she. She was upset with me at first, but six months later she called and told me I was right. She was grateful that I stood my ground. I was grateful that she agreed that it was the right decision.

I was able to focus completely on my training. I stayed with Alan and Alison for three weeks. I got a job at the Copley Price YMCA, a new branch that opened in San Diego. And I got my first studio apartment that same month. It was nice having my own space for the first time in my life. It was also weird. I had no one to blame if the place was dirty. It was all my fault if the dishes were in the sink or there was water on the bathroom floor.

I didn't have much—a full-size bed, a television, which sat on the floor in my room, a two-seater couch, and some towels. I wasn't home much anyway. I was either working or training. I just needed a place to lay my head at night.

I sold the PT Cruiser to my sister Gina's mom, who needed a car. And Alan turned around and surprised me with a car for my birthday—a Toyota RAV4. He also sat me down and taught me about managing money, budgeting, and saving. Besides school, that had to be the most valuable lesson I could learn, as valuable as our first swim lessons together.

"I want you to be able to take care of yourself, by yourself," Alan told me. "Of course, Alison and I will always be there for you, but you need to stand on your own."

I learned quickly that between my own place, gas, and food, a paycheck in San Diego wouldn't go very far. It took me a whole year of leaning on Alan and Alison to be able to carry my weight. I figured out how to save for the things I wanted and give myself some breathing room, which again, was hard in pricey San Diego. But I did it. It gave me some perspective on the sacrifices that my mother had made. I was supported by her and CAF, Alan and Alison, and I still struggled. I could only imagine her resilience.

As I learned in my swim training, having a team makes it easier.

I decided to move in with Rudy, who had a house in Spring Valley. It was an athlete's pad. I decided when the lease was up on my studio, I would move in there. But by at time, Rudy had moved to Colorado Springs to prepare for the Rio Olympics. Blake, an African American Paralympic runner, also moved, so I was moving in with two new roommates—one who was preparing for the

Olympics in track and the other, a former track athlete who was training for a triathlon.

I was working full time and swimming doubles—in the mornings with Alan, and with a local swim team in the evenings. My two-a-day training allowed me to drop three seconds off my time in the breaststroke. I was ready for the next level!

The Pan Pacific Championships are held every four years and rotate between the four Pan Pacific charter nations, the United States, Canada, Japan, and Australia, and has divisions for both able-bodied and para-athletes. It was in the United States in August 2014, in Pasadena, California.

At this meet I would see how I stacked up against the international competition. I felt very new, very green despite my training. For the warm-ups, the organizers told us to circle-swim. I was familiar with it because of my training with my teams. We were all making adjustments. In some countries, the circle swim was in the opposite direction.

There were swimmers in our events who were missing arms, missing a leg, and visually impaired. I was the only above-the-knee double amputee in each of my races. There were coaches speaking different languages, with different-sounding English accents. I was on the verge of sensory overload, but for the past couple of years, I had practiced with several teams in crowded pools and had to navigate all that. I had learned how to apply what I knew from my training. I just had to focus and stay in my lane.

Nerves aside, I was prepared.

I recognized one of the dudes in my race. His name was Raphael. He had beaten me so badly at the Paralympic trials in

2012 in London, that when I saw him, I was instantly mad because of the memory. I couldn't stop thinking about it. Here he was again.

When we lined up and that gun went off, I must have blacked out. Because when I hit the wall at the finish, I was by myself. I swam the way I knew how, controlling my movements and breathing. After what felt like forever, I came up. First place! I beat that dude by three seconds. It was so satisfying. Little four-year-old Malia was in the stands with her sign, cheering the loudest and telling everyone, "That's my brother!"

I swam the 100-meter breaststroke and came in first. The first time I got gold!

I also swam for Team USA in the medley relay. I swam the breaststroke in the second leg. We got the silver medal. I also won the bronze at the 2015 PanAm Games, where I experienced traveling as a USA athlete through the athlete village. I loved being among the other elite athletes.

And the wins had me on such a high, I thought I was ready to go to the nationals and then the Olympics. I thought.

Despite all my training, I didn't qualify for Paralympics in 2016. The trials are based on time, and you're graded on a curve. The fastest guy in my class was so much faster than me that even though I had a decent time, it wasn't good enough. The 100-meter breaststroke was my main event, and I was out on day one! Once I didn't make it, I didn't want to be there. I checked out.

I went home disappointed. I was living paycheck to paycheck in an expensive city, sharing a house with a terrible roommate (the other guy was really cool but not cool enough to make up for the terrible one).

I needed a change. I had applied several times to the Paralympic resident swim team in Colorado, and I was rejected each time. I applied again and didn't tell anyone, just in case the answer was no again. Rudy had joined the team right out of high school when they first started a resident swim squad. He worked his way from resident team member (where I'd be starting if accepted) to the national team, where he received a salary, health benefits, and the whole nine yards. Rudy had since moved on to New York. His agent had gotten him a gig there and a few endorsements. He was doing well. That's where I wanted to be.

Weeks later, I finally got the call that I'd been accepted to the national team residency. I told Rudy, and he offered to go with me to make sure I got settled in. He knew all the people and wanted to set me up to win.

"Let's drive to Colorado!" Rudy suggested. I was down. I was always down for an adventure. He was going to stay in Colorado with me for a couple of weeks and then drive to New York from there. This was in December 2016, and I was to start with the team top of January.

I packed up my car, though I didn't have much stuff. Rudy flew in from New York and got his car from his home in Riverside. He packed up what he needed for New York, met me in San Diego, and we rode caravan-style to Colorado.

I love road trips. Whenever I went on a long ride, Rudy and I would call each other and talk or let the other know it was time for a pit stop. He was playing his music. I was playing my music. We were together and in our own world at the same time.

The journey was a thousand miles going north on I-15 and east on I-70. Driving through Colorado was a scary new world. There were signs like "Watch out for falling rocks!" And they meant that. I had never really seen mountains until I came to Colorado Springs. Everything that I *thought* was a mountain in Alabama was actually just a hill. San Diego had mountains, but not like this.

When we arrived at the Olympic and Paralympic training center, the biggest, most state-of-the-art facility I had ever seen, Rudy had access to everything. We checked in. Rudy had his own room, and the staff showed me to mine. After dropping off my things, I headed right to the cafeteria, where they had every kind of food you could imagine.

I loved this place. They even had a recovery center with plunge pools and hot tubs. And the best training equipment ever. This facility housed both Paralympic and Olympic athletes. Hanging with athletes from different sports was amazing. I was even working out with Olympians from the Summer and Winter Games!

Claressa Shields was there. She won gold medals in the women's middleweight division at the 2012 and earlier that year at the 2016 Olympics, making her the first American boxer to win consecutive Olympic medals. She's from Michigan and no joke! It was cool to see her there. I loved being around the other boxers. Their coach, Coach K., let me work out with them. (Watch out for my left jab!)

I spent more time with the able-bodied athletes than my own teammates on the swim squad. They were very curious about the disabled athletes. They were in awe of what we could do. And of course, we were in awe of them, mutual respect.

I had a more difficult time fitting in with the Paralympic swim team. It started the first day when the coach told us he lived in Jamaica teaching for three years, and he hated it there. What kind of person could hate Jamaica? Jamaican food was my favorite cuisine, and I loved the music and, of course, the people. That was my first red flag. The team seemed to be half filled with spoiled, entitled, privileged people. I think the coach thought I would fit in, but I didn't feel like I could talk about anything outside of the sports, or the sacrifices my mother and I had had to make to be there. The few times our paths crossed at CAF events, we were both very cordial. But now that I was living with these people and dealing with this coach on a daily basis, I was miserable. He thought he was getting a Carlton Banks, but I was really more like a Will Smith or Jazzy Jeff. And becoming more of a Malcolm X. I had very little tolerance for the baked-in bigotry, and I was less and less interested in appeasing them when they made offhand comments. It didn't help that in the pool, I wasn't improving.

Coming off a great couple of years when I was able to shave seconds off my time, I was now finishing in the middle of the pack. I was there training for the 2017 World Championships in Mexico City, which would be my first. This was going to be the tee-up to the Olympics. After my performance in the Pan Pacific Championships, I just knew I was going to crush it.

Instead, I got crushed. I came in seventh in the 100-meter breaststroke—which was supposed to be one of my strongest events. I didn't swim my best race. I was too heavy. I was injured. But I also knew, even healthy and lighter, I wouldn't get much faster—not fast enough to come in first. *I wasn't built for swimming*, I thought. Great swimmers—able-bodied or para—are long and lean. Rudy is built like that. So is Michael Phelps. I'm thick and muscular. And as I got older, my body was filling out, not slimming down.

We did win a bronze medal in the freestyle relay. Robert, who had cerebral palsy, swam the first leg. I swam the second. Ty, a single below-the-knee amputee, was third. He and I trained together. Zach was the anchor. He was a little person.

Although I wasn't feeling my team, I was loving everything else—including Colorado Springs!

I had some decisions to make.

Chapter Eighteen

NEW YORK, NEW YORK . . . A HELLUVA TOWN!

IT WAS 2019 AND MY YEAR SEEMED TO BE GOING WELL. I WAS featured in *Men's Health* magazine in the March issue. I got a call from CAF to move to New York and help build their presence in the city. The World Series for Paralympic Swimming was happening in Indianapolis. A good showing in the World Series would all but guarantee an athlete a spot on the 2020 Paralympic Games in Tokyo.

I had been struggling with the Paralympic community for a while, swallowing the slights and the personal limitations. And I was frustrated with swimming with my team. I was used to being around different people from different backgrounds. I had been to college. I had traveled and lived in different places. But I was swimming with a community of people who were used to being coddled and in many ways, were very sheltered. I felt like an outsider. If I decided to go to the World Series, I was making a commitment that I couldn't see myself staying with—at least not happily.

I had a choice to make. Go to New York and start a new path or finish what I started with the Paralympic journey?

New York was not a place I ever imagined living. I had visited there when I was seventeen years old while competing in a CAF event. But I found the city too crowded, too loud, and too chaotic. San Diego, where I'm from, is a big city, but New York is another world.

I spoke with Rudy, who had already moved there. CAF enlisted him a year before. He was from the desert of California, and I remember him also saying that he would never live in New York. But there he was, thriving. "It's actually not so bad," he told me. "I'm starting to like it." Rudy lived in Crown Heights, Brooklyn. And if he said New York wasn't so bad, I believed him.

"Okay," I said. "Can I crash on your couch until I get on my feet?"

"Sure!" he said. "The more, the merrier."

I arrived in New York during the best time—the summer. It was better than I expected. Rudy had built a little community, and I fit right in. He lived in a three-bedroom apartment on Nostrand Avenue in Brooklyn. He had two roommates—one of whom was scheduled to move out in a month. The plan was for me to sleep on the couch and move into the bedroom when his roommate left. He didn't leave for three months. We were cramped, but I tried to stay out of everyone's way.

Rudy took me around the neighborhood and introduced me to some of his friends, took me to events. I got to experience my first-ever West Indian Day Parade Carnival. It was right outside our door. The morning of, the entire neighborhood was buzzing as people were busy prepping for one of the biggest carnivals in the world—a couple of million people were expected to descend on Eastern Parkway to watch the floats go by.

We left the house around noon and walked right into sights and smells, colors and sounds. There were steel drums and reggae music booming everywhere. Haz, one of Rudy's friends, took me with him to check out the neighborhood. He walked me into this woman's apartment—a stranger—for a plate of food.

The spices—curry and jerk—were literally wafting through the air. "You can't just go in someone's place like that, can you?" I asked.

"Today, we can!"

Man, the oxtails and rice and peas were some of the best I've ever had! I fell in love with West Indian food and West Indians that day. The floats were amazing, all the different nations represented on this day. Trinidad and Tobago. Barbados. Jamaica! And the women dressed in colorful Carnival costumes having the best time dancing through the parade. Whew! I could not have moved to New York at a better time. It reshaped my whole experience.

Back at home in San Diego, colorism was real. I was often made to feel different because of the darkness of my skin. In Brooklyn, I was appreciated. The women paid me attention in a good way. I felt loved. In New York, since there were so many different kinds of people, I was just a guy. I wasn't the disabled guy or the handicapped guy. No one paid any attention to my disability—especially on the streets. There was too much going on to worry about the guy with the prosthetics. People had told me how rough New York is. But I met some of the nicest people there. New Yorkers aren't to be messed with, and they definitely don't suffer fools, but they are some of the most interesting and unique people out there.

The famous song says if you can make it there, you can make it anywhere. But I felt like I had a head start on most because I'd made it out of shelters in California and Alabama. New York was going to be a piece of cake.

When Rudy's roommate finally moved out, I moved into my own room. It was small but perfect. I mastered the subways in no time, taking the 2 or the 3 train into Manhattan every day. There were very few stations that had elevators or lifts, so I had to take the stairs in the mad rush of people. Going down was no problem. My prosthetics had sensors and hydraulics that allowed me to navigate the steep stairs without holding on to the railing. But I always held on, just in case. Coming up out of the subway was more of a chore. I have a more than six-foot wingspan, and I could hold on to both sides of the railings at once and hoist myself up like a rope climb, skipping two and three steps at a time when there was room.

I got a job at Tailwind Endurance. It was a training facility for individuals in endurance sports. I coached swimmers. We had an Endless Pool, where I would give one-on-one training sessions. After my training sessions, I could hop in the Endless Pool and get in a workout myself. But I really liked the JCC down the block because they had a big, beautiful pool where I could do real laps.

I also started running in Central Park. I heard that's where the New York City Marathon's final three miles took place. I wasn't much of a runner, but I wanted to run that iconic race one day. I'd start with doing just one lap around the park—six miles. It took me a couple of months to get that one lap around, and just in the nick of time, I got an opportunity to race in a half Ironman. Running around Central Park every day gave me the confidence to say yes.

CAF asked me and Rudy to speak at a fundraiser in Oceanside, New York. They were also holding a half Ironman on Sunday and asked us both to compete. I was excited because I had never been there, and the landscape was beautiful. We had to talk at the fundraiser on a Saturday, and we both decided to participate in the half Ironman on Sunday.

The event had both relay teams and individuals, abled and disabled. Rudy and I both opted for the relay, separate teams, and we both had a proxy rider for the biking portion. I didn't have a bike and Rudy hated riding. He would use a standard bike, pedaling with his prosthetics. It was painful and it was the bike that kept him from making history in the Ironman Triathlon in Hawaii a year before.

I had never competed in anything like this. For the relay, the organizers gave us trackers that we had to pass off to our teammates when we finished our leg.

I hit the water, trying to keep up with Rudy, who is probably the best swimmer I have known. He's built for the water. I couldn't keep up. He finished three minutes before me. I finished the 1.2 miles in thirty-three minutes and handed off my tracker to Big. Big Sur was a donor who volunteered to race the bike portion for me. He lived up to his name. He was big and strong.

Rudy and I went to the waiting area for our teammates to come in. Big Sur came in before Rudy's guy, handed me the tracker and I took off running. I thought I would hit a wall or get tired, but I didn't. I had never in my life run thirteen miles, but I finished with such a good time that the organizer of the race asked me if I wanted to compete in the Ironman.

"In Kona?" I said.

"Yes."

While I killed this Oceanside race, surpassing everyone's expectations (including my own), Kona was double the distance, and I had less than six months to train. *And* I didn't have a bike! There would be no Big Sur or relay partner in the Ironman. I would have to do this race on my own.

"We can find you a bike," said Bob, the cofounder of CAF.

"I think you should do it!" Rudy encouraged me.

Why not?!

Chapter Nineteen

GRABBING THE BATON

My participation in the Ironman came about because someone paved the road for me to run it. Of course, there was Rudy. But there was also Jon Franks, who was shattering the norms before I was born. In 1988, Jon Franks arrived in Kona to participate in the Ironman Triathlon. He had his sights set on becoming the first paraplegic to finish the race but was told he would not be allowed to race.

"This isn't your usual kind of race," said Valerie Silk, president and then-chair of the Ironman.

She believed his wheelchair would be a risk for him and for the able-bodied athletes.

"The run is one of my biggest concerns," she told reporters. "When the sun goes down in Kona, it's like the lights turn off in the whole world. It's just not safe to have people in wheelchairs going 15–20 miles an hour on the road when you have people wearing reflective gear and shaking cups of ice to try to be heard by the other runners out there."

Jon Franks wasn't buying it. He saw it as "extreme discrimination." He had finished an Ironman in St. Croix in thirteen hours and no one was hurt or hampered by his wheelchair.

"I'm not sure what the bottom-line motivation is for putting me off," he said. "I think they really just don't want to take the time or the consideration to mess with it."

Silk said she wasn't "willing to let someone else run their race in the middle of our race. I don't feel the Ironman is under any obligation to provide a stage for the promotion of personal goals."

It wasn't a personal goal for Jon Franks. He was simply opening the door for all of us.

He showed up the next year and somehow made it into the water. A couple of friends snuck him in, and he finished the 2.4-mile ocean swim. And he wasn't last, either. He was prepared to continue but as he was headed to his handcycle to start the second leg, he was stopped by two guards, who escorted him from the race.

"God knows, I would do it their way if I was on my feet," he said.

Jon Franks was born with legs, unlike me and Rudy. He recalls waking up in the hospital after a motorcycle accident and being told he would never walk again, paralyzed after being hit by a truck in 1988 and breaking his back and pelvic bones, among others. He made a vow that day that he would end up doing something unbelievable despite the prognosis. He would do an Ironman! By 1994, Jon Franks had competed in more than thirty triathlons globally.

And after several tries, he was finally allowed to race at Kona—becoming the first paralyzed athlete to compete in the Ironman Triathlon.

He backstroked the 2.4-mile swim in a wet suit. His crew was waiting for him at the shore with his handcycle when he finished. His handcycle looked like a wheelchair. It was close to the ground and had twenty-one gears with a hand crank in front of his chest. The 112-mile, zigzagging, hilly course proved too much for Jon, and he was unable to finish. But he proved it was possible.

The very next year, John Maclean finished the race! He was the first wheelchair athlete to complete the Kona Ironman. He went on to become the first paraplegic to swim the English Channel and won the silver medal in the 2008 Beijing Paralympic Games.

In 1988, Carlos Moleda beat John Maclean's Ironman record by a whole hour. (That same year, Jim MacLaren set the record for single-leg amputees in the Ironman World Championships. CAF was started to help him get an accessible van after his second accident that made him a quadriplegic, paralyzed from the chest down).

Moleda, a former Navy Seal, was paralyzed while on a mission in Panama, where he was shot in the back and leg during an ambush. "In the beginning, you think this is temporary. In my mind, it was like in a few months, I will go back to work. And then when you realize this is for the long term, you really reassess your life. You go through adjustments; some will take a lifelong to fully understand," Carlos said in an interview. It was during physical therapy that his therapist signed him up for a wheelchair race. He was hooked on the competition.

In 2009, Rudy became the first double-above-knee amputee to finish an Ironman Triathlon (the Ford Ironman in Arizona). But Rudy did not complete Kona.

If I finished, I would become the first. I was determined.

Chapter Twenty

THE LAST LEG

RIDING INTO THE TRANSITION AREA OF THE RACE, I FELT instant relief. I did it! I finished the bike portion. That was more important to me than finishing the whole race in that moment. This was the leg that took Rudy out of the race. And he and Bob, cofounder of CAF, were very nervous about how I'd do in the bike portion. I could tell that they didn't believe I would finish, either. And since they were anxious about it, so was I.

I completed the 112 miles of biking in a little under nine hours, a full thirty minutes sooner than expected and thirty minutes ahead of being disqualified from continuing on to the run. What was crazy was that I did it without my tracker. I was so hurried getting out of the water and grabbing everything I needed for the bike that I left the stopwatch behind.

As I was pushing up the hill for mile two of the bike, I saw Bob in a near sprint. He ran a mile and changed to catch me and give me the stopwatch. He knew where I would be—everyone did. You could search for any racer's number and follow them. I wore bib number 430. Bob knew I would be struggling up this hill. It was a monster. If I stopped pedaling, the bike would surely roll down. So, I was pushing. He caught up to me.

"You're going to need this," Bob said through heavy breaths.

"Thank you!" I said.

I rolled into the transition area and was greeted by an ecstatic Bob and an even more overjoyed Rudy. All of us felt utter relief. I was given ten minutes to get ready for the run. I sat in my cycle for a couple of minutes, collecting myself. My body was stiff and sore. My handcycle didn't come with shock absorbers, and the road was rough. Every bump, every pothole, every bit of that hard service shot through my body and landed in the small of my back. It was on fire.

I let Bob pull me out of the bike, and I unfolded myself. I shook out my arms, which had been pedaling almost nonstop for nine hours. My biceps, triceps, and forearms were shot. I was looking forward to running and giving them a rest.

Rudy brought me my blades. My stumps were slightly swollen. I had to squeeze into my prosthetics. It was a tight fit, but when I stood up, I appreciated being on two legs. I raised my arms over my head and did a few deep stretches, leaning side to side and back.

I drank some electrolytes, ate a Snickers bar that was in my pack, shook out my arms again, and headed off to tackle the 26.2 miles to the finish.

Rudy gave me a speech before I started the run.

"Take the first ten to eleven miles slowly," he said. "You will be going through town and there will be a lot of people there. Don't let them gas you up to go faster. Take your time. Pace yourself."

I nodded in agreement. I had every intention to follow his plan.

I started out the first couple of miles just bouncing along, my pogo rhythm. *Bounce. Bounce.* My hips were opening. *Bounce. Bounce.* My lower back was loosening. *Bounce. Bounce.* By mile three, I was feeling good.

We were literally running through the streets of Kona—past shops and restaurants and bars and apartment buildings. There were people everywhere, cheering. My adrenaline was flowing. When I got into the heart of town, that crowd absolutely gassed me up, and I did the exact opposite of what Rudy instructed me to do. I took off!

I was set to be featured in an NBC Sports special, so there were cameras filming from helicopters above. There would be people on motorcycles filming as well as a truck that was following along. The cheering crowd was made for TV, and I wanted to give them a show.

I was excited and I was running as fast as I could. In the window of one of the bars along the road, I spotted a man I met the night before standing on a chair. He was a podcast host and was quite a character with his ukelele. He stood on his chair with a beer mug in his hand. He saw me and raised the mug, cheering me on. I waved back.

I also saw a family I had met in the lounge area of the hotel the night before. The dad was competing, too. He was there with his wife and daughter. They had all wished me luck. His little girl, who was around six years old, had never seen an amputee. She couldn't stop staring and asking questions. I didn't see the dad during the race, but at mile 4 of the run, there was the little girl and her mom. Their faces lit up when they saw me. They had a video recorder and were ready to film the dad when he came by. I ran over to them and gave the little girl a high-five. She was thrilled. I waved to the mom and kept going.

I did a lot of promotion leading up to the race to let people know that I would be there. It was one way to keep the opportunities flowing in. There were quite a few people on the sidewalk who recognized me and a few who were there just to see me! It was a lot to take in.

The first eleven miles were a blur. I ran those miles on pure adrenaline and excitement. With 15.2 miles to go, I hit a wall, *the* wall.

The sun was setting. Rudy told me that when it got dark is when I would have to dig deep. "You're going to want to quit," he said. "But you can't!"

I watched the sun dip down behind the mountains of Kona. I'd started the day watching the sun come up over the ocean. Now I was watching it go down, and still I had more road ahead of me than behind to complete. I slowed down to a walk to take it all in. Also, I didn't have much energy left in my tank, having spent it on the first eleven miles. I was tired.

There were fewer runners on the road now. Many had dropped out, some had already finished, and most were ahead of me on their way to the finish line. I found myself once again alone. And in the dark.

We were told to have glow sticks and bells because nighttime on the roads on the outskirts of Kona Island was pitch black. I was thrilled initially at the thought. I wanted to experience being in the pitch of night without the glow stick to guide my way. I wanted to see how far my instincts, focus, and training could get me. But the transition from running in a business area to a residential area with houses, to a remote, rural space with nothing around us was an adjustment. Still, Kona at night was another kind of beauty. It was quiet. And it wasn't pitch black after all. The moon was bright in the cloudless sky and lit my way.

I now had twelve miles to go as I rounded the loop back to the transition area. I was still walking on Queen K Highway—named for Ka'ahumanu, one of the favorite wives of Kamehameha, the first ruler of the Kingdom of Hawai'i. I read up on Hawaiian history before coming here, and I learned that upon the king's death, Ka'ahumanu assumed rulership along with the king's son. She was known as one of the most powerful queens in Hawaiian history.

The Queen K Highway led to the airport, which was the race route's turnaround point. When I saw the signs for the airport, I had hope. I fought through the wall. My spirits picked back up and I pushed forward. *Bounce. Bounce. Run. Bounce. Run. Bounce.*

At the airport turnaround, I saw Sika Henry. She was on the other side, finishing as I was heading into the last eleven miles. Sika is an ultramarathoner and the first Black woman to professionally compete in and complete an Ironman triathlon. This was the first time I got to see her, and it was as she was finishing her race. As we passed each other, I yelled, "You got this, Sikka!"

"Oh my God," she said seeing me. "You got this, too!"

That exchange propelled me even more. It was just the boost I needed.

Ten miles to go.

And there was Rudy. He had on his running legs. Technically, it's illegal to have a guide or someone running with you, unless you sign up for a guide at the beginning of the race. Had I done that, my run would be considered "assisted." I didn't sign up for a guide. And I had no idea that Rudy was going to run with me. He was there at each transition to make sure I had everything I needed. Rudy flew in just to be there for me. He coached me. He let me know how I was doing on time. He also told me what I needed to finish each particular leg. Now he was here to make sure I finished.

He knew that these next ten miles would be the hardest. It was exactly ten years prior that Rudy was on this very course and didn't make it. But he was here now for me. We made eye contact. I saw him in his running blades. I saw the smirk on his face; I pumped my fist in the air, and I said, "Let's go!"

We said nothing for the mile that we ran together. At the mile nine marker, he ran off the course. We bumped fists before he left and he said, "See you at the finish!

Rudy told me it was going to get darker and quieter. I was going to end this race the way I started in the wee hours of the morning in the dark—alone.

The mountains to my left were obscuring the moon. When the sun was setting, the colors bursting through the mountain were magnificent. Now there was blackness. I saw nothing but an occasional glow stick in the distance. I heard bells jingling from time to time. And there was the patter of feet in a rhythm. And winded breathing. No cheering. No talking. Heavy breathing and the pitter-patter of feet occasionally as a runner would pass me.

I thought I had hit my wall and come through it miles back, but I learned that the *real* wall was ahead of me. Mile 20! Rudy had warned me as I was training that I would hit a second wall.

"Once you think it hits you, it won't be it…it's still coming," he said. I didn't believe him. But boy did I hit that other wall hard! I wanted to just drop and stop.

There was a little boy at the aid station at mile 21. As I was now in a slow bouncy walk, I heard a voice shouting, "Red Bull! Red Bull!" Volunteers at the aid stations at each mile handed out orange slices, Coca-Cola, Gatorade, and Red Bull. (I'm sure there must have been water there, too.)

"Red Bull!"

That kid was hopped up on the Red Bull. He couldn't have been more than eight years old, but he had the energy of twenty kids. It became a rallying cry for me.

"Red Bull!"

When he saw me, he ran to give me a Red Bull. I passed the aid station, laughing because I could still hear him yelling, "Red Bull!" as I kept going. That little boy helped me break through my wall.

The science and research station was the next landmark that

told me I was nearing the end. It was a long stretch. The sun was all the way down and the moon was glowing. Kona looked like a whole different island at night. Houses lined the mountains, lights flickering in the distance.

I slowed again to a walk to take it in. This was a once-in-a-lifetime experience. I could now see cars on the sidelines, recording. Helicopters flew overhead. NBC was following me. Finish or not, I was being filmed. It was a special moment that I'd be able to watch back.

I got through the pain and now I had another issue—time! *Oh my God, am I going to finish?* I thought.

Officials in the cars were yelling for me to run.

I started the race doing seven- and eight-minute miles. I was now down to doing a mile in twenty minutes. At this pace, I would exceed the seventeen-hour limit. I had six miles to go, and I was doing my best. There were a lot of people now coming to the loop. I started to get sad and feel defeated. But I still had to try. I'd come this far. Did I really want to go home after having done more than twenty miles? No, but did I have enough left in the tank to finish?

I had heard talk of a lot of spiritual forests in Hawaii. I heard stories of tourists taking rocks from sacred places on the beach and ending up with curses on their lives. This island takes care of itself, they say. The elements work with each other. I noticed it with the wind. While it was tearing me up during the swim and the bike, it was at my back now—pushing me to the finish line.

Three miles to go, and I could feel a back spasm coming on. *No!* The wear and tear on my body was real . . . but I also knew the mind can go places the body cannot. I was hungry and hurting—but not quitting. There are people who walk days to escape tyranny, with no food in hand and no idea where the next meal is coming from. They cross borders to get away from dictators and terror. They do this with nothing. I knew I could get through three miles.

I dropped my head and took off. In the time it took for me to drop my head, I heard a huge shout. I raised my head to see where the shout came from. I didn't see anyone. Perhaps the island was shouting for me to keep going.

So I did.

———

In addition to Bob and Rudy coming to support me, there were thousands of people following me on social media, pulling for me. My mom was at the finish line, waiting. I was not letting them down. I was into hour 16. It was dark and I was alone.

I later learned that my mom was a nervous wreck at the finish line as hundreds of runners finished the race and I was nowhere to be found. She was afraid something had happened to me. And she also knew I had to finish in seventeen hours for it to count.

With thirty-four minutes to spare, I came hopping around the bend on my blades, heading for that finish line. My mother was on her feet, her smile wide enough to rip her face. She was jumping for joy as she saw me. Seeing her gave me a new surge of energy I didn't believe I had. I lunged for the imaginary tape at the finish line and crossed it with my arms raised in the air—just like I envisioned in the mirror. Almost an entire day had passed.

"Are you okay?" my mother whispered as she gave me the biggest hug in the world. That hug was really holding me up.

"Yes, yes." And I meant it. Fewer than .01 percent of the world's population have finished an Ironman Triathlon.

I finished!

Epilogue

NEW LEG, NEW BEGINNING

AFTER FINISHING THE IRONMAN IN OCTOBER 2019, I SPENT the rest of the year and the first few months of 2020 on a major press run. CAF was so proud of what I had accomplished that they had me all over the country. I was speaking and appearing at events. My life was suddenly hectic. I spent a couple of weeks in California, where Rudy was training, and we decided to take another road trip, this time to New York! We were still paying for the loft on Nostrand Avenue in Brooklyn, so we decided to go back, continue our work with CAF and figure it out.

We rented a car and hit the road. It was three thousand miles, three days on I-80, stopping at rest stops and sleeping in the car to save money. We ate a lot of fast food and listened to good music. As we got off Route 78 from Jersey City onto the Manhattan Bridge into Brooklyn, I knew I wouldn't be in New York long. I loved New York. But I was longing for Colorado Springs.

After my performance in the bike leg of the Ironman, I was leaning toward training for the Paralympics in cycling, and Colorado Springs was the best place to do that. Compared to the business of New York, Colorado Springs' mountains, hills, thin air, and empty roads would be perfect. And my sister Gina said I was a better person in Colorado. "You so much more chill," she said. And she was right. There was a calm and peace in my soul there.

Before moving back to Colorado Springs, I spent a couple of weeks volunteering with a nonprofit called Limb Kind Foundation in a children's hospital in Ethiopia. That experience was life changing. Being in Ethiopia—one of the few nations to never be colonized by a European nation—was amazing. And the children in the hospital were so beautiful. Many had missing limbs, like me, and they were fascinated by me, as I was with them.

I was letting my hair grow out around this time. I was feeling like the corporate look wasn't who I was. A couple of the older girls asked if they could braid my hair. I had never had my hair braided before and was surprised when they told me that I had enough to braid.

I didn't realize how spiritual that experience would be. I started studying how certain African nations used braids to send messages. If the hair was braided up, that was for war. Braided down was for peace. The styles I would sometimes see in images of ancient Africans weren't for fashion or beauty, I realized. They meant something.

Leaving Ethiopia, I decided I was going to honor that tradition. I was still in New York, and I was looking for a braider there. It's Brooklyn, so there were hundreds of braiders, but they were all too expensive. I was soon to be between jobs, and I couldn't blow that kind of money on hair. So, I rocked the patted-down 'fro for a minute.

I decided to go to Colorado Springs in March 2020 while the news cycle was predicting that cities would be shutting down because of COVID-19. I made it there, and the next week everything—the entire world—shut down. I was grateful to be in Colorado Springs, one of the most beautiful cities in America, during COVID. I had time to think and process and grow. At the beginning of the summer of 2020, I headed to Florida to stay with one of my favorite aunts. It was also one of the few states that probably never shut down. We took a mini-vacation to the Florida Keys, where I ended up butt naked in the ocean.

On the drive down to the Keys, I told my aunt about my experience in Ethiopia and how I was thinking about moving to Colorado Springs…and how I was thinking about growing locs.

"I think locs will be too much to manage in the water," I said, getting her opinion. She knew everything about hair.

"Why don't you try brother-locs," she suggested.

I heard of sister locs, but I don't think I ever saw anyone rocking brother locs. She said they were gaining popularity.

As I floated in the ocean on my back that day, naked as the day I was born, I was never so free. I made my decision right there that when I got back to Colorado Springs, I would find someone to do my hair. It would be another layer of freedom.

I googled "Brother Locs" in the Colorado Springs area and found two locticians. I reached out to both. Miss Mia returned my call. She and her husband were from New York, and they were so nice. I felt instantly at home in her shop, and she charged *a third* of what they were asking for in New York. "Can we use your photos in the shop to promote?" she asked when she was done.

Of course! I was so happy with the job she had done.

The next time I came several months later, she had my picture up everywhere, including one of me from the Ironman Triathlon. She was proud to have me as a client. That second time, I saw a woman, one of her clients, who was finished and leaving as I was coming in. I noticed her immediately because she was beautiful. I played it cool, smiled and said hi before taking my seat in Miss Leah's chair.

She smiled back. *Wow!*

As she was doing my hair, Miss Leah was telling me about a Black History event she puts on every year for the community. She invites speakers to come and inspire the people. She asked me if I would be a speaker. I couldn't tell her no.

I arrived at the event and went to sit on the stage with the other panelists. There were two other speakers. And there she was—the woman I met in Miss Leah's shop. Her name is Ahsaadyia, and she was invited to talk about the law and her career in criminal justice. Ahsaadyia had all my attention.

If I'm being honest, the first time I laid eyes on her, I knew. That was it. And when I saw her sitting on that stage, something about the way she was sitting, how she carried herself, totally captured me. I knew we would get to talk when the speakers' portion was over. I played it cool, while Ahsaadyia spoke before I did. I locked eyes on her the entire time. And she was smiling. That's when I got tongue tied. That smile!

After the event, we exchanged numbers. And we haven't gone a day without speaking since. She has helped me grow into the kind of man that I want to be in terms of a partner. The way I thought about marriage and a man's role before Ahsaadyia was very rigid and traditional. Now I think about it as a partnership. My partner and I do everything *together*. We're both capable of doing everything by ourselves, so when we come together, we are doing what we do best and making it easier for the other. I like to cook. But Ahsaadyia is a better cook. She was raised by Jamaicans. Her seasoning game is definitely on point. They say food is the way to a man's heart...it's true. Especially for me. After the first meal she made for me—curry shrimp, rice and peas and peppers and onions—I said to myself, "I *have* to cherish her!" Like I had to do with athletics, it's taken practice. Meeting Ahsaadyia was just the starting line. And this love is a race I have plenty of time to run.

Our dream is to have a farm where we raise our children. We are looking for land. Ahsaadyia has moved careers from criminal justice into agriculture. We will carve out some space for my mom, too. I can't wait! I told her she better get a lot of rest over the next couple of years because when the grandbabies come, we're tapping her in.

My mom has been through a lot. After I went off to college, she found herself—I later learned—back in a shelter. She was struggling emotionally with my leaving and was having a hard time being stable. But she's comfortable now. She's finally giving herself time to know herself and focus on what she likes and what she wants from this life. When I think about the course of my life, I see a young man who had every possible obstacle stacked up against him. I've had to overcome not only people's expectations of what I can do but also the limitations I put on myself. My mother always pushed me to be my best, and as a result, I'm living a life I could never have imagined, and she is too. She allowed me to see the possibilities. She deserves the same. We all do. Because it's never too late!

Acknowledgments

I would like to extend my deepest gratitude to the following individuals who have played pivotal roles in bringing this book to life:

First, to Karen Hunter, thank you for your unwavering brilliance and dedication. Your hard work, expertise, and passion for storytelling have made this project a reality, and I am beyond grateful for your guidance and support every step of the way.

A heartfelt thank you to Ian Kleinert and Betsy Berg, whose belief in me and this story helped open the doors to this incredible opportunity. Your encouragement and collaboration have been invaluable throughout this journey.

To Hachette Publishing, thank you for providing me with the platform to share my story. Your faith in my voice and your commitment to making this book a reality means more to me than words can express.

Finally, to my mother, Marian Elaine Jackson, your example of strength, love, and unwavering support has been the foundation

ACKNOWLEDGMENTS

of everything I have achieved. You are my rock, and I am forever grateful for the love and encouragement you've given me in pursuit of my dreams.

With deep appreciation and gratitude,
Roderick Urise Sewell II